EXPLORING THE GREAT RIVERS OF NORTH AMERICA

CALLIOPE — THE *MISSISSIPPI QUEEN*

Built especially for the steamboat, it ranks as the world's largest steam-powered piano.

EXPLORING THE
Great Rivers
OF NORTH AMERICA

NATIONAL
GEOGRAPHIC

WASHINGTON, D. C.

CONTENTS

PRECEDING PAGES: RIO GRANDE
Milky waters of the Southwest's longest river—roughly 1,900 miles—pass the limestone hills of Big Bend National Park, Texas.

OPPOSITE: SUSQUEHANNA
*Kayaker negotiates Sheets Island archipelago, a state-protected natural riverine area near
Harrisburg, Pennsylvania, on the East's longest non-navigable river.*

NATURE'S HIGHWAYS across a continent, the rivers of North America are many and varied. But what makes a river great? Size matters, of course, both length and volume. So does a river's role in human history. Rivers link us to a given landscape, dividing yet also uniting as they run from mountains to the sea, providing corridors through which we access interior areas. Certainly the Missouri qualifies as a great river: Physically large *and* historically significant, the storied pathway of Lewis and Clark and of countless others headed west.

A much less obvious candidate, Virginia's James River, is tiny in size—but a major player in terms of history. This is why *Exploring the Great Rivers of North America* includes the James but not, say, the far larger Saskatchewan.

A second consideration in planning this book was to focus on main streams and avoid tributaries. Thus, we feature the Mississippi—legendary "Father of Waters"—but not the Ohio.

Third, this book defines each river narrowly, following geographic convention rather than tracing it to its most distant watershed. So it is that the Missouri begins at Three Rivers, its nominal starting point, rather than with Red Rock River, its physiographic headwaters.

ARCT

OCEA

Yukon

U.S.
CANADA

Fraser

Columbia

PACIFIC

OCEAN

Sacramento

San Joaqu.
River

TROPIC OF CANCER

ARCTIC CIRCLE

Labrador Sea

Hudson Bay

Nelson

La Grande

Saskatchewan

CANADA
U.S.

Mississippi

St. Lawrence

Susquehanna

Hudson

ATLANTIC OCEAN

Missouri

Platte

Ohio

James

Arkansas

Savannah

Mississippi

Brazos

Colorado   Featured river
Fraser   Other river

0   400 miles
0   600 kilometers

o Grande

U.S.
MEXICO

Gulf of Mexico

RIVERS TO TH

■ RIVERS SEAM NORTHEASTERN North America, defining its past, enriching its present. Like the timeworn landscape itself, the rivers here are old, cutting broad, easy swaths hospitable to humans and their ways. For 10,000 years now, people have thrived on these rivers and their resources. Native cultures were well established along their shorelines long before Europeans began bearding the Atlantic and using these rivers as conduits into the continent. The French and English and Spanish planted their first settlements along river shorelines, and, like the natives, marveled at the abundance that surrounded them. "Heaven and earth never agreed better to frame a place for man's habitation," Capt. John Smith rhapsodized as he explored Chesapeake Bay and its tributaries, the James, Susquehanna, and others. And to Jacques Cartier, the plentitude along the shores of the St. Lawrence made it "as fine a country...as one could wish, covered...with the finest trees in the world."

To all those early adventurers and the generations that followed them, North America's eastern rivers, their shorelines, and their resources were meant to be exploited. In New France, the *coureurs des bois*—fur trappers and traders—followed the St. Lawrence and its tributaries far inland, seeking as many beaver pelts as possible. Though their motive was largely greed, they also explored much of the continent along the way.

Down the entire eastern seaboard, rivers allowed early commerce to burgeon. On the James, planters grew rich floating hogsheads of tobacco downriver to ships bound for Europe; loggers deep in the interior mined

ATLANTIC

■ *K.M. KOSTYAL* ■

wilderness forests and sent their timber treasures to market on the Susquehanna, the St. Lawrence, and the other great estuaries.

As the colonial era ended and ambitious new nations coalesced on the continent, the very flow of many of the major eastern rivers was diverted to fuel progress. Complicated canal projects channeled rivers around their natural rapids, allowing mule-drawn barges to move passengers and goods up as well as downstream. In his dreams of commerce for the fledgling country, George Washingon envisioned a Great Central American Walter Line, a series of canals that would link the James to the Ohio to the Mississippi and on and on to the Rocky Mountains.

Though Washington never lived to see any of those canals completed, he surely would have applauded the monumental channelization success of the 20th century: the St. Lawrence Seaway, a gateway between the Atlantic and the vast inland sea of the Great Lakes.

As this century draws to an end, a new attitude toward rivers is emerging. Humans have come to realize that rivers are not endlessly exploitable, eternally renewable, or ever invulnerable. The St. Lawrence can be overfished, the James and Susquehanna can become diseased by pollution. Rivers, in fact, are more than mere conduits for commerce. They are living organisms. Their histories, their legends, their moods, their very movements texture human life. In the last century, Henry David Thoreau wrote, "He who hears the rippling of rivers in these degenerate days will not utterly despair." His words ring even truer today.

ABENAKI INDIAN—ODANAK, QUEBEC *Adorned for a contemporary powwow, Jake "War P*

...lieu continues the traditions of his Abenaki ancestors, who lived along the St. Lawrence and south, into New England.

ST. LAWRENCE

HEADWATERS—LAKE SUPERIOR

■ TO THE NATIVE AMERICANS who lived along it, it was "the walking road," a tide-swirled aquatic highway—endlessly bountiful, dangerous, immense. To the Québécois of today, the St. Lawrence remains an immense fact of life. Not simply a river—a *rivière*—but something bigger. They call it a *fleuve*. And where it widens out downstream, it becomes *la mer*—the sea. More than 20 miles across in places, a thousand feet deep just offshore, it surely can feel like an arm of the sea, its dark, quick currents interrupted by the shimmering arc of a whale's back or the bobbing heads of seals.

Like most things immense and legendary, the St. Lawrence has no exact beginning or ending. Some geographers trace its source to the St. Louis River, deep in the American interior at the western corner of Lake Superior. By this calculation, the river melds with the Great Lakes for more than a thousand miles before exiting the northeastern end of Lake Ontario. Now indisputably the St. Lawrence, it threads between Canada and the United States, following a fault that opened about 6,000 years ago in the ancient rock of the Canadian Shield. Its flow as reliable as the lakes that feed it, it swirls past the wooded islets and summer homes of New York's Thousand Islands, past the grain fields of Ontario. As it drops toward sea level, it occasionally broadens into shallow lakes or narrows into rapids that once made it unnavigable. But since 1959 the canals and locks of the St. Lawrence Seaway have smoothed its rough edges. Now, the skyscraper-like bulks of oceangoing ships squeeze through this watery rift in the continent, shuttling between the Atlantic and the Great Lakes.

So where exactly does the St. Lawrence end and the Atlantic begin? Geographers cite a place about 600 miles downstream from Lake Ontario. Pointe-des-Monts, a wind-whipped cape, marks the north shore here. On the south shore, fishing villages of the Gaspé Peninsula face the sea, the Appalachian Mountains rising at their backs. It is here, geographers say, that the watercourse broadens, the Laurentian Current sweeps in from the Gulf, and the river gives way to the sea.

With a little imagination, you could say the look of the downstream riverscape hasn't changed dramatically since 1535, when French explorer Jacques Cartier sailed up this great river. He wasn't the first. The Montagnais and Iroquois had been here for hundreds of years before him, fishing, hunting sea mammals and game. When Cartier asked his Iroquois guides what body of water he was on, they told him simply "a river without end." Cartier may have believed them, since he never did get to the end of it. But he did plow a good distance upstream, awed by what he saw. In the river were "very great numbers" of fish "as large as porpoises" and "white as snow"— beluga whales, still seen on the river today.

It was early September by the time the French band reached a large St. Lawrence Iroquois camp, known as Stadacone, on the north shore of the river. Later French would call it Quebec. The chieftain Donnacona, "Lord of Canada," gave the explorers a ceremonial welcome, and Cartier felt safe enough to leave his two larger ships here, as he continued upstream in lesser craft. "We found many houses along the banks of the river," he wrote, "the people at the time busily engaged in fishing." On October 2, Cartier reached yet another large island, this one holding the impressive Iroquois settlement called Hochelaga. More than a thousand people had gathered to give the French "as good a welcome as ever a father gave to a son." Anxious for a vantage of the area, Cartier climbed the island's summit. From there he could see the distant Appalachians, the Laurentian Highlands hugging the north coast, and in between "the most beautiful land, arable, smooth, and plain"—the St. Lawrence Valley. He named the summit Mont Royal, which in time became contracted to Montreal.

On an early October day almost half a millenium later, I too stood on Mont Royal and took in the vantage. The autumn skyline was crenellated by the artifacts of 20th-century industry: office towers, occasional smokestacks, the monoliths of the University of Montreal that now top Cartier's Mont Royal. But in the distance, the river cut an unperturbed, steel-gray path beneath the overcast sky. Its blessings to this particular spot have been many.

Thanks largely to the St. Lawrence, the old Iroquois settlement of Hochelaga has become Canada's second largest city, its streets as international and ethnically diverse as any in the world. But above all else, Montreal is a port and center of transport. For centuries, it was the natural endpoint of the navigable St. Lawrence. Above it, the river became obstreperous with rapids. In an attempt to outmaneuver nature, Montreal's Lachine Canal opened in 1825, extending the navigable waterway another eight-and-a-half miles. Its diverted waters powered mills, turbines, waterwheels, winning the area acclaim as the "cradle of Canadian industry." Finally, in 1969-70, with the St. Lawrence Seaway claiming most upriver traffic, the Lachine shut down.

Now filled in and carpeted with grass, the old canal area has made the transformation from gritty portside to chic *Vieux-Port*. Weekenders come to picnic along its riverfront or browse and dine in its old warehouses, reborn as upscale restaurants, shops, and inns. Across the river, the occasional ship inches through the easternmost lock on the seaway. Downriver, the seaway no longer funnels through a man-made canal, but instead follows a dredged channel in the river.

Just as in the days when Iroquois ruled the riverfront, the 150-mile stretch of the St. Lawrence between Montreal and Quebec is lined by an almost continuous chain of villages, some still arranged loosely around an old church whose belfry once served as a landmark for passing ships. Downriver from Montreal, the river breaks its usual confines, splaying out into shallow, wind-churned Lac St. Pierre.

At the east end of this lake, the St. Maurice River joins the St. Lawrence, and the smokestacks of Trois-Rivières announce the world's pulp-producing titan. The town grew rich off timber a century ago, its factories fed by the vast Laurentian forests. But long before timbering made men wealthy, there was fur. The early Europeans in Cartier's wake came as *coureurs des bois*, fur traders and trappers. Following the tributaries of the St. Lawrence, they paddled far into the interior, searching for the beaver pelts that all Europe wanted.

CARTIER'S ARRIVAL — 1535

Romanticized in this 19th-century painting, Jacques Cartier and his men explore the St. Lawrence. Though the Iroquois initially welcomed the French, colonists later found themselves embroiled in the century-long Iroquois Wars.

In 1608, more than 70 years after Cartier's reconnaissance, Samuel de Champlain established the first trading post on the river, near the old Iroquois village of Stadacone. Champlain's simple habitation eventually gave rise to one of the most charming cities on the continent and the capital of the province: Quebec City.

If Montreal's character is big, international, and forward-looking, Quebec's is small, decidedly French, and devoted to the past. Plain-faced Norman buildings front the few streets of its historic Lower Town, wedged into rock-rimmed Cape Diamant at gull's-eye level, just above the St. Lawrence. At night from Lower Town, you can hear migrating snow geese calling to each other on the river, narrow and fast-moving here.

More developed and boisterous in character, blufftop Upper Town has been dominated for a hundred years by the almost fortress-like bulk of the Château Frontenac.

From this famous hotel, a promenade parallels the river, leading to what seems at first glance to be a quiet city park fringed in autumn by maple reds and oak golds. But this is no park. It was here, the Plains of Abraham, where the decisive battle between France and England for control of Quebec took place on September 13, 1759. England's Gen. James Wolfe prevailed, defeating Gen. Louis-Joseph de Montcalm. Several years later, the 1763 Treaty of Paris ceded all New France to England.

"You know, the English and New Englanders tried to take Quebec several times," Pierre Desrosiers, an archaeologist with the provincial government, tells me as we walk the blufftop promontory. "In 1690, Sir William Phips from Boston sailed up the St. Lawrence with a small armada to attack the citadel here. When he sent a messenger to governor-general Frontenac demanding surrender, Frontenac replied that he would answer 'through the muzzles of my cannon and muskets.' He did too, and the New Englanders were repulsed. Phips lost several of his ships to bad weather on the way downriver. We've recently located the wreck of one and begun salvaging it. The St. Lawrence is littered with wrecks because the strong current creates treacherous conditions. But it's rare to find a wreck of such age and well-preserved condition."

From the Quebec narrows just below the city, the river begins to broaden dramatically as it sweeps past the Charlevoix coast. Every small hamlet here has a resident

SETTLING THE ST. LAWRENCE

Long a natural thoroughfare, the St. Lawrence gave rise to a procession of villages bordered by rangs—long, narrow plots of land that permitted each farmer direct access to the river. Remnants of the rangs still etch some river landscapes today.

artist or two, drawn to the fast-changing dance of clouds and sunlight reflecting on the sea, and the shadowed tumble of hills that rush down to meet it. The Charlevoix and the coast road end abruptly at the Saguenay River, a true fjord whose tentacles reach far inland. No bridges, only a ferry, cross the mouth of the Saguenay to the remote wildness of Côte-Nord, or north coast, where forest-edged lakes glitter in rock basins and the St. Lawrence remains ever present.

Once the home of sea-savvy whaling and sealing families, the scattered communities around the village of Tadoussac today gain more from whale watching than whale hunting.

At Cap-de-Bon-Desir, you can stand on low boulders almost at sea level and see fin whales, belugas, sperm whales, minkes—even the biggest of all, blue whales—glide by.

"I came here a few years ago to camp by the coast and I saw the whales," Marie-Thérèse Bournival, a longtime Montreal journalist, told me. "From my tent, I could hear them spouting just offshore. It was so remarkable and the place so beautiful that eventually I moved here." She now directs Archéo Topo, a museum and archaeological center that sits on a point of land overlooking the St. Lawrence. Devoted to the north shore's Native American past, the center also coordinates with the newly established Saguenay-St. Lawrence Marine Park. Not just an underwater sanctuary, the park encourages locals to get involved, and they do, enthusiastically. Locals like Rosaire Otis.

The wind shoves fiercely at us from the northeast as we stand at the Archéo Topo dock while Rosaire readies his boat. Winter comes early to Côte-Nord, and already the October morning air cuts like a thin, frozen knife. But we are undeterred. Rosaire Otis agreed to brave the weather and take us out on the St. Lawrence. He tells me—in French, with Marie-Thérèse translating—that we probably won't see whales. "The sun is at the wrong angle," Marie explains. "Rosaire says we won't be able to see very well along the coast here, with the sun shining off the water." Now nearing 60, Rosaire learned as a boy to think like a whale. His family (of 19 children!) were among the last hunters on the coast, surviving off beluga and seal. "We traded seal meat for groceries," he explains. "They're fabulous creatures," he adds, with French passion. "I am in love with the seal. But still, each year I take one. It's in my blood. The challenge of it—the hunt, the sea, maneuvering around the ice. The sea is beautiful, always, but it can destroy in a moment."

As Rosaire predicts, we see no whales our first hour out. We head back, spotting two whale-watching Zodiacs at idle. Clearly the local Essipit Indians operating the boats have sighted something. We pull up nearby and wait, but after a few minutes the Essipit and their passengers lose patience and roar off. Rosaire is undeterred. He pulls out a harmonica, declaring playfully, "Whales like my music. This will bring them close by." Minutes later a telltale mist hisses near the boat. "Here she comes," Marie-Thérèse whispers, as a fin whale rolls its gray back up from the sea, so close that we can almost breathe into its blowhole.

One, two, three rolls and the whale dives deep into the heart of the St. Lawrence—a vast submarine dimension below the flat blue surface sheet we see. Whatever we call it—river, fleuve, sea—we'll never know it the way that that whale does. ∎

OLD QUEBEC CITY, QUEBEC

Grande dame of the St. Lawrence, the Château Frontenac hotel dominates Quebec's blufftop Upper Town, while below it cobbled streets and picturesque shops texture Lower Town. In 1985, UNESCO designated this city North America's first urban world heritage site.

THOUSAND ISLANDS, NEW YORK—*Just downstream from Lake Ontario, the St. Lawrence embrac*

centration of roughly 1,800 isles and islets, some topped by getaways as extravagant as Boldt Castle, on Heart Island.

LOWER ST. LAWRENCE — TADOUSSAC, QUEBEC

Flowing west to east farther than any other North American river, the St. Lawrence widens downstream from Quebec City, becoming an arm of the sea by the time it reaches Tadoussac (above), some 2,000 miles from its Lake Superior headwaters.

EISENHOWER LOCK — MASSENA, NEW YORK

Challenging human senses—and expectations—a freighter slowly navigates part of the St. Lawrence Seaway while cars tunnel underneath it (opposite). An engineering marvel, the Seaway's system of canals, locks, and dredged channels officially runs 2,342 miles, from Duluth, Minnesota, through the Great Lakes, to the Atlantic. Along its course, 15 different locks enable ships to ride out a 572-foot difference in elevation.

ÎLES DE LA MADELEINE — GULF OF ST. LAWRENCE

*"As for fish, this is their kingdom…. The big river is full of sturgeon, salmon, shad, pike, turbot,"
marveled a French missionary in 1636. Today, faced with lower harvests, St. Lawrence fishermen
struggle to maintain a livelihood that sustained their forebears for generations.*

FOLLOWING PAGES: ÎLES DE MINGAN — EASTERN QUEBEC

*Bound for the broad Atlantic, a freighter passes a gunsight notch formed by the rocky
Mingan archipelago, north of Anticosti Island. Ahead lies Cabot Strait — separating the island
of Newfoundland from Nova Scotia — and, finally, the sea.*

SUSQUEHANNA

DUGOUT CANOE—OTSEGO LAKE, NEW YORK

■ STORIED, CANTANKEROUS, ANOMALOUS, the Susquehanna seems to contradict itself endlessly as it loops through the eastern heartland. At 444 miles— most of them through the center of Pennsylvania—it ranks as the Chesapeake Bay's largest tributary, contributing fully half of the bay's fresh water. But it also bears the dubious distinction of being the continent's longest non-navigable river. A river of small towns and big dreams, it has managed for most of its length to thwart human attempts to control it, canalize it, or make it an inland conduit to the sea. Nothing but the pleasant little town of Havre de Grace marks the Susquehanna's entrance into the bay. Upriver about a hundred miles, the Susquehanna's personality splits in two: The West Branch burrows into the rugged wilds of the Appalachian Mountains, while the meandering North Branch cuts its own course through history and geography.

Despite its navigational contrariness, the Susquehanna is as quintessentially American as any river in the country. The redoubtable John Smith first "discovered" it while reconnoitering the upper bay in 1608. Waterfalls, which his band named Smith Fales, kept him from sailing far upstream, but he did meet the local Susquehannock Indians. "Gynt-like people," he called them. "Such great and well proportioned men are seldom seene." Their language, Smith rhapsodized, fit their proportions, "sounding from them, as a voice in a vault." Perhaps because the people were so impressive, the river came to bear their name. Never anglicized or truly tamed, the Susquehanna River seems to this day to have kept its native character.

Even at its source, it is an American classic. The longer North Branch officially begins at New York's Otsego Lake, whose glimmering charm inspired native son James Fenimore Cooper to reincarnate it as Glimmerglass Lake, the setting of his epic Leatherstocking Tales. Natty Bumppo, Cooper's quintessential hero, rejected the white man's ways and wiles, choosing to live close to nature in Susquehanna country, like his friends the Mohicans. Cooper's own father, William, had put the lake on the map by establishing the prosperous lakeside village of Cooperstown in the 1780s. A later Cooperstown resident, Abner Doubleday, ensured the town's immortality by—according to legend—inventing the great American pastime here. Today, pilgrims flock to the town's Baseball Hall of Fame; relatively few venture the couple of blocks down to the lakeshore to see the Susquehanna, which Fenimore Cooper called "one of the proudest rivers of the United States," start its long journey to the sea.

Admittedly, the river exits the south end of the lake as no more than a knee-deep stream only a few feet wide. Yet even before there was a town here, the Susquehanna's inauspicious size nearly thwarted dreams of imperialism. A small marker by the lake explains how Gen. James Clinton assembled a force of some 1,800 men and more than 200 supply boats at the lake in 1779. He planned to float his entourage downstream, southwest to Tioga. There, he would join Gen. John Sullivan's troops on the "Big March" that would sweep the area clear of Senecas, Cayugas, and their French allies. But the Susquehanna's scanty flow did not comport well with Clinton's plans. He built a dam across Otsego Lake and waited a full month as its level rose. Then, boats at the ready, he destroyed the dam, and on the resulting tidal flood his entourage raced downriver. Unhampered by dams these days, the North Branch inches along through farms and forests of the hill-pleated Appalachian Plateau. At the old factory town of Binghamton, the river becomes wider and more fulsome and stays that way as it turns south into Pennsylvania.

The Pennsylvania town of Towanda fronts the Susquehanna, its substantial Victorian homes stairstepping up the hillside from the river. You can tell as soon as you drive its streets that, in an earlier age, industry thrived here. At the local historical society, period photographs immortalize the boom times, when transportation, logging, leather tanning, and coal made men rich. Down at the river, you can still see vestiges of the long-defunct North Branch Canal, one of several star-crossed canal projects along the Susquehanna. Fearful of losing trade to New York's Erie Canal, the Pennsylvania legislature funded a massive public-works program in 1826, hoping to make the Susquehanna a major conduit of trade, both to the south and to the west. Canals were begun here on the North Branch and along other runs of the river. But ravaging spring floods and low summer water made these costly projects ultimately ineffectual; railroads soon made canals obsolete. Efforts to tame the Susquehanna proved such a phenomenal fiscal flop that Pennsylvania verged on bankruptcy.

Today, with heavy industry giving way to tourism, local boosters have renamed the region watered by the Upper Susquehanna the Endless Mountains, in deference to the Appalachian Highlands that roll on and on here. The forests, too, seem endless, particularly in the remote north-central sweep of the state, where the West Branch of the Susquehanna makes a prolonged and ragged bend. Timber barons in the mid-19th century sent legions of loggers into the wilderness to mine its riches and float the harvested logs downriver. Williamsport became the timber capital of the West Branch, its streets bristling with the opulence of new money.

Those were not the days of conservation, yet the devastation from overlogging was so severe that it spawned concern for the land even then. "There are few places in the east where the natural beauties of mountain scenery and the natural resources of timber lands have been destroyed to the extent that has taken place in northern Pennsylvania," a U.S. Geological Survey reported at the end of the 19th century. "One may journey for miles without encountering a mature tree."

Today, the signs of humankind lay easier on this land — occasional modest towns, half-pint hamlets, and private hunting clubs, no more than cabins at the end of a dirt road. And on a horseshoe bend in the river stands one of those curious remnants of early America — the scattered cabins and gridded streets of a failed utopia.

French Azilum grew up in the 1790s, after a group of French exiles, having escaped their country's bloody, head-rolling revolution and an equally bloody slave insurrection in the French West Indies, established their own Parisian-style outpost here. Neatly laid out, their village was never very big, but it did sustain a kind of *haute societé* here in the middle of the Pennsylvania wilderness. In the evenings, expatriates would assemble at the Grande Maison, a huge log affair, disporting themselves as if at a palace ball. With the fickleness of nobility, however, the citizens of French Azilum gradually lost interest in playing pioneer. After Napoleon's rise to power assured more order and fewer rolling heads, they abandoned their utopia beside the Susquehanna and returned to France.

Lashed into a makeshift barge, big timber from northern Penns-

It took Yankee hardihood to knuckle down and make the Susquehanna home. As early as the mid-18th century, Connecticut Yankees had been filtering west toward the fertile lands watered by the Susquehanna. Many settled in the Wyoming Valley, near present-day Wilkes-Barre. They fought Pennsylvanians and Iroquois for their rights to this farmland, as rich as any in the country. And in 1778 many of them died in an infamous, retaliatory attack made on them by Indians and Tories. Ironically, the Wyoming Massacre only perpetuated the romance of the Susquehanna. Scottish poet Thomas Campbell's 39-stanza epic, *Gertrude of Wyoming*, inflamed European imaginations

28

with both the tragedy of the massacre and the pastoral glories of the Susquehanna.

> Delightful Wyoming! beneath thy skies,
> The happy shepherd swains had nought to do
> But feed their flocks on green declivities...."

A century later the happy shepherd swains had disappeared from the Wyoming, replaced by waves of Welsh, Irish, German, and Central European miners. A newly industrializing nation had discovered that below the valley's green declivities lay the world's largest known deposits of anthracite coal. Five hundred square miles of it seamed northeastern Pennsylvania, and running across the surface like a ready-made highway was the Susquehanna. By the 1870s hundreds of collieries lined the North and West Branches of the river. Pastoral no more, the sweet Susquehanna country had became a nightmarish place of smudge-faced workers, towering black culms of mining refuse, Molly McGuire boys fighting hard for workers' rights, and coal and iron bosses battling right back. Like the people along it, the river suffered during the decades of intensive mining, particularly as acid drainage from bituminous fields seeped into its western streams.

SUSQUEHANNA—MID-1800s

downriver towards Williamsport, a 19th-century lumbering center.

Though pollution and mounds of mining refuse still scar the riverscape, the Susquehanna has begun to recover. "Every year, the fish—bass, chubs—move a little farther upriver," Dan Devlin in the state's Department of Conservation and Natural Resources, tells me. "Even the spring run of shad is returning, thanks to lifts and ladders that get them over the four dams at the lower end of the river, near the bay. And the state is acquiring more and more of the thousands of islands in the river, to preserve them for recreation and natural habitat. We get huge numbers of migratory birds—snow geese, swans, warblers, great egrets—on the river in spring and fall. We want the river to be hospitable to both wildlife and people. The Chesapeake Bay Foundation has even developed a River Island Trail that leads boaters up the river."

At Northumberland, the West Branch, having plowed 240 miles east from just outside Carrolltown, joins the 324-mile-long North Branch to form the main stem of the Susquehanna. Its broad brown surge, sometimes a mile across, courses past forested islands and small towns. A screen of trees follows its shoreline, and wading birds peck along the shallows or glide overhead. The serene riverscape is interrupted only briefly by Harrisburg, with its ornate dome of the state capitol.

Ten miles downriver, the Susquehanna's most notorious landmark, an ominous hourglass-shaped stack, squats in mid-river, its reactor cooled by river water. Three Mile Island is really only about two-and-a-half miles long, but that's a quibble. No one would quibble with the public fear its nuclear facility provoked in late March 1979, when America thought it might be facing the doomsday scenario of a meltdown. Though the day was saved, Three Mile Island—both its name and image there on the river—continues to instill dread.

It's difficult to connect that strange tower with the consoling silos, patchwork fields, and tradition-bound lives that persist almost in its downriver shadow. For 200 years the Old Order Amish and Mennonites of Lancaster County have faithfully preserved a lifestyle they consider ordained by God. Their horse-drawn carriages roll past farmland held by the same families for generations. Their bearded, solemn men with broad-brimmed hats stave off the endlessly probing tourist stares, while their women look shyly away. Like Quakers, Moravians, and other persecuted sects that began settling southern Pennsylvania in the early 18th century, these "Plain People" came seeking a sturdy land and a place where they could worship and live as they saw fit. A central tenet of that worship is a rejection of the "profane" outside world and its technological trends. Life goes on here as it has for centuries, broken only by the invasive drone of tourist traffic plowing back and forth on the country roads between Lancaster, Bird-in-Hand, and Intercourse.

Despite their non-violent ways, the Amish have had to wage a determined war to keep their lifestyle alive. A 1972 Supreme Court ruling finally and forever sanctioned their approach to schooling, which ends with eighth grade. "A way of life that is erratic but does not interfere with others is not to be condemned because it is different," Supreme Court Justice Warren Burger wrote in the decision.

And so the Amish are safe along the banks of the lower Susquehanna. In its time, the river has harbored a lot of "erratic" lives—French nobility dancing away the wilderness night; Quakers fleeing persecution and Yankees seeking new land; immigrants willing to bury their days in underground coalfields to buy a new life; and an imaginary, leather-stockinged white man who preferred Indian ways to those of his own kind. Susquehanna country sustained them all in their time, and their stories belong to the river. ■

AMISH BUGGY—LANCASTER COUNTY, PENNSYLVANIA

In tune with the past, one of the world's largest communities of "Plain People"—Amish and Mennonites— dwell along the Susquehanna, following lifestyles little changed since they left Europe 200 years ago.

BINGHAMTON AREA, NEW YORK *Pastorally perfect farms color the Susquehanna River*

e New York, just upstream from where the river's North Branch begins its long, looping descent into Pennsylvania.

HARRISBURG, PENNSYLVANIA

Taking root on the Susquehanna's generous banks, Pennsylvania's state capitol boasts a tiled dome, here shrouded by scaffolding necessary for a recent renovation. Englishman John Harris first recognized the commercial potential of this island-laden section of the river, establishing a trading post and ferry here in the early 1700s. A century later, in 1812, Harrisburg's central location helped it best larger Philadelphia to become the capital city of the state.

ROCKVILLE BRIDGE—NEAR HARRISBURG

At 3,280 feet, graceful Rockville Bridge ranks as the world's longest stone-arch railroad span; it has withstood the Susquehanna's seasonal floods and tempers since 1902. Railroading made Pennsylvania an industrial powerhouse during the 19th century, quickly surpassing the state's tentacled and obsolete canal systems. These days, however, the river sees more canoe traffic than commercial cargo.

FOLLOWING PAGES: NEAR MARIETTA, PENNSYLVANIA

Forested banks and islets of some stretches of the lower Susquehanna recall virgin woods that once blanketed the entire state-and made the river valley a haven for migratory birds and other wildlife. Loggers decimated Pennsylvania's trees during the last century, prompting a backlash that gave rise to an enduring conservation movement.

JAMES

VIRGINIA TOBACCO PLANTATION

■ "THIS RIVER WHICH wee have discovered is one of the famousest Rivers that ever was found by any Christian."

So wrote English adventurer George Percy as he sailed into the James in the spring of 1607. To me, 350 years later, the James was simply the landscape of my childhood, no more famous than the street I lived on. Almost daily I walked the shores of its endpoint, Hampton Roads harbor, watching a parade of freighters, destroyers, and aircraft carriers negotiate its four-mile-wide froth. To the east the river rounded Old Point Comfort, joined with the Chesapeake Bay, and then with the Atlantic. To my young eye, all the adventure of the world lay just around that point. That this river was an adventure in itself escaped my wandering imagination.

Negligible in size by great-river standards, the James never leaves the confines of Virginia. Yet in the 340 miles it takes to spill out of the Allegheny Mountains, cross the Shenandoah Valley and Blue Ridge, then vein the Virginia Piedmont and Tidewater, the James manages to compact the history of a nation. America was birthed here, fought its wars of survival along these shores, watched its age of industry and its rise to military superpowerdom ride the tides of the James.

George Percy and his English compatriots had no way of foreseeing such a future when they sailed into the lower Chesapeake almost 400 years ago aboard that now famous, three-ship caravan — the *Susan Constant*, the *Godspeed*, and the *Discovery*. At the first estuary that presented itself, the English turned west and headed upstream, naming the river they were on after their king — James I. For two weeks they continued upriver, exploring and feasting on abundant oysters and wild strawberries. The river, wide and substantial, had a deep and steady flow. Where it narrowed, about 30 miles upstream from its mouth, the English discovered an island propitiously surrounded by a channel so deep they could moor their ships to trees on its shoreline. It would make a good place for a fort, James Fort. A safe spot, relatively speaking, where they could protect themselves should the local Powhatans pester them from land or the Spanish come at them from the sea.

Today, the tentative toehold they established ranks as the oldest permanent English settlement in America. Every schoolchild knows the story of Jamestown: The early "starving time" that almost drove the colonists to abandon the settlement, the courageous exploits of John Smith, the equally brave deeds of the Powhatan princess Pocahontas. We know that after a struggle, brief by historic standards, the English prevailed—against both the wilderness and the native Powhatans. By 1620, the trans-plantation, or "plantation," of English empire in America had taken root along the James.

Smith, who had returned to England after only a year and a half at Jamestown, never truly left it in his mind's eye. It became his obsession, and he touted its virtues to anyone who would listen. "Adventure to those faire plantations of our English Nation," he proclaimed, promising that one would "see how many rich and gallant people come from thence, who went thither as poore as any Souldier or Sailer." The shores of the James did indeed offer largesse in those early, opportunistic years. Tobacco turned Jamestown and its satellite plantations from struggling enclaves to boom towns in whose very streets the "stygian weed" was cultivated.

Jamestown survived as the colonial capital until the end of the 17th century, when the capital moved inland to Middle Plantation—Williamsburg—and Jamestown lapsed. Old James Fort was assumed to have drowned long ago, taken as the river clawed away at the island banks. But in 1996, archaeologists found remains of a small palisaded enclosure at the edge of the shoreline. Inconsequential when compared to the bulk of the continent behind it, James Fort was substantial enough to ensure that English culture would be permanently grafted onto American soil.

More impressive remnants of that culture still front the river upstream from Jamestown Island. The "distressed cavaliers"—royalists fleeing Cromwell's England in the 1640s—found a welcome home in Virginia, and a phalanx of their baronial estates still overlooks the James. At Virginia's oldest plantation, Shirley, tradition remains a tangible thing; descendants of its original Hill and Carter families have lived amid its Georgian splendor since it was built in the 1720s. Near Shirley Plantation, a line of centuries-old poplars frames Westover, the elegant home built by urbane planter William Byrd II. He well understood the opportunities to be mined along the shores of the James, and his diary for September 19, 1733, notes that on that day, he "laid the foundations of two large Citys. One…to be called Richmond, and the other at the point of Appamattux River to be named Petersburgh." Byrd's Richmond would become the phoenix of the South, reinventing itself time and again.

Today, Richmond's jagged halo of high-rises leaps up unexpectedly just at the fall line of the James, where rapids begin. In this century, the city has rediscovered tobacco, with major players in that industry headquartering themselves here. But such prosperity is a New South phenomenon; the Old South still hangs like a tracery of fine lace about the city. After all, this was the capital of the Confederacy, and even now, along the marshy lowlands at the city's edge, you can see abandoned workshops of the long-defunct Tredegar Iron Works, whose furnaces almost single-handedly supplied the southern army. Not far away lies Belle Isle, a small island that was hardly belle. Once crammed with as many as 8,000 Union privates, it ranked as one of the most notorious prisoner-of-war camps ever to sully American soil.

In those long years of conflict, much of the river became an artery of war. At its lower end in Hampton Roads, one of the greatest naval battles in history took place early in the war. On March 9, 1862, newly minted ironclads—the C.S.S. *Virginia* (Northerners called it the *Merrimack*) and the U.S.S. *Monitor*—squared off in a four-hour contest that ended in a draw. Several weeks later, the North's "Napoleon"—George McClellan—used the James to launch his Peninsula Campaign. Sailing into

RICHMOND, VIRGINIA—BEFORE THE CIVIL WAR

Idyllic in its antebellum charm, Virginia's capital city profited from its James River location, particularly after the completion of the Kanawha Canal (center) in the 1850s. A waterborne highway linking Richmond with lands to the west rich in produce, coal, and iron, the canal and its mule-drawn packet boats also became a fashionable means of travel, far cleaner and quieter than stage or steam trains. Recently rebuilt, a mile-long stretch of the old canal continues to thread Richmond's shoreline.

Hampton Roads with almost 100,000 men, he landed at Fort Monroe, whose moats and casemates still anchor the tip of Old Point Comfort. From here, McClellan marched cautiously up the Virginia Peninsula to Richmond's door. But that was as far as he got. He was never able to get inside, and after the Seven Days' Battle in early summer of 1862, he gave up and retreated to Harrison's Landing, south of Richmond on the James.

"My father was a drummer boy with McClellan," Malcolm Jamieson told me a few years ago. We were sitting in his gazebo, on a sweep of lawn overlooking the river. "When he learned this place was for sale 45 years later, he came back and bought it." The "place" Malcolm was referring to was Berkeley Plantation, on the rise above Harrison's Landing. A stone's throw from Byrd's Westover and of the same vintage, Berkeley has probably seen more history than any other spot on the river. Colonists celebrated their first thanksgiving on this land in 1619; the later redbrick manor house was built in 1726 by Benjamin Harrison, signer of the Declaration of Independence; his son, President William Henry Harrison, was born here; one of McClellan's generals, Daniel Butterfield, composed "Taps" here. Jamieson himself, who died in 1997, spent his long life restoring Berkeley to its former splendor. He was an owner worthy of history.

Above Richmond and the fall line, the James changes character dramatically, becoming a rural, meandering river that gets lost in pastures and woodlands. In this countryside near nothing, one of the country's last poled ferries—actually a two-car barge propelled by pulleys and guided by a ferryman wielding a pole—moves back and forth between the riverbanks, trying to avoid the rambunctious weekend tubers who float the river by rubber.

"The James's upriver rapids may not rank as more than Class II by today's river-running standards, but you try maneuvering a 40-foot bateau down them," Jeff Taylor, a TV programming director in the Lynchburg area, told me. Every July, he and a cadre of other bateau enthusiasts take a week off from the 20th century and experience the James in an armada of home-built boats that re-create the flat-bottomed river freighters of the 19th century. Floating downriver from Lynchburg, they reenact the lives of the old river runners, who braved the rapids to transport flour, hogsheads of tobacco, and other products to Richmond. "Mornings, we start out early, when there's a mist still hanging on the river and it's almost silent. Just the sounds of animals— wild turkey, deer, sometimes a bear. It's life on the river as it was meant to be."

If George Washington had had his way, the James would have become part of the Great Central American Water Line, his ambitious plan for linking the Atlantic to the Rocky Mountains by a series of canals. That, of course, never happened, but by 1851 the James River Canal had made it 197 miles inland, crossing the Blue Ridge and entering the Shenandoah Valley at the town of Buchanan. One of its 90 locks, now restored, still breaches a low point in the Blue Ridge; it recalls the 19th-century belief that canals could surmount all natural obstacles and ensure American prosperity.

But canals were obsolete almost from their inception and quickly succumbed to the Iron Horse. It would take a railroading robber baron to forever put the James on the map of American industry. Collis Potter Huntington first saw the river as a young traveling salesman in 1837. Its lower end as it spread into Hampton Roads seemed a perfect site for a major port, and yet it was no more than a sleepy fishing village. Some 40 years later, Huntington returned, the port vision still in mind. By the mid-1880s, he had extended his Chesapeake and Ohio Railroad from the riverbanks at Newport News all the way to New Orleans—and railroading was only part of his scheme. In 1886, Huntington opened the Newport News Shipbuilding and Drydock Company. More than a century later, the shipyard's cavernous buildings still sprawl along the southern shoreline of the James, the sounds of their industry echoing out across the river.

"I worked in the shipyard my whole life. Started there when I was 14 as a messenger boy," 93-year-old Everett Benton tells the story, always with pride. "My boss told me I looked like a hard worker, so he'd sponsor me. Everybody wanted to work for the shipyard in those days. Fathers worked there, and their sons and grandsons after them. For fifty years and seven months I worked there. I saw a lot of great ships built during that time."

As a child growing up on the James in the 50s, I took the shipyard as I took the river: for granted. Periodically, the neighborhood would collect on the shores of the river to watch as one of the Newport News-built behemoths, newly christened and launched, moved majestically downriver and out to sea. The supercarriers *Enterprise* and *Yorktown*, and the luxury liner *America* made that four-mile trip from the James down Hampton Roads to the Chesapeake. And they were only a few among hundreds of others.

Now, as then, the Newport News shipyard constitutes only part of the military might concentrated in the area. On the south shore of Hampton Roads lies Norfolk Naval Base, largest in the world. Even in these post-Cold War days, this is the place to "see some Navy"—from nuclear subs and tenders to destroyers and carriers, some 150 different ships call this their home port. I don't know how their crews feel as they round Old Point Comfort into Hampton Roads, their ships riding high on the waters. But I still see the James from water level, with a young eye. To me, such ships will always be those enormous barriers we had to tack around when we were out sailing. And the river itself, for all its history, seems an almost visceral creature, its tidal flats scenting the air with a salty pungence, its whitecaps churning up their own excitement.

A great river from any vantage, the James. ■

JAMESTOWN SETTLEMENT, VIRGINIA
Armed and costumed as a 17th-century English colonist, a reenactor greets visitors to historic Jamestown, site of North America's first successful English colony.

NEAR THE HEADWATERS *In a quiet pocket of Virginia's Allegheny Mountain.*

...son and Cowpasture Rivers merge to form the James, an ancient river that has run for some 600 million years.

RICHMOND, VIRGINIA *Torched at the end of the Civil War, Richmond and its business district glitters ane*

...he banks of the James. A flood wall built in the 1980s protects the low-lying riverfront from the stream's periodic ragings.

SHIRLEY PLANTATION — CHARLES COUNTY, VIRGINIA

Shirley, one of the great James River plantations, and others of its era still grace the historic stretch of riverfront located between Richmond and Williamsburg. Aspiring to bring English elegance to the American frontier, 18th-century colonial planters, grown rich on tobacco, wheat, and slave labor, spared no expense in building and decorating these Georgian showplaces, which, with their outbuildings, functioned as villages unto themselves. As William Byrd II, colonial diarist and the owner of stately Westover Plantation, put it, "Like one of the Patriarchs, I have my Flocks and my Herds, my Bond-men and Bond-women...so that I live in a kind of Independence on every one but Providence."

COASTAL WETLANDS — TIDEWATER VIRGINIA

As it heads toward Chesapeake Bay, the James feeds tidal Virginia's seemingly endless marshlands (below). Traditionally, its bountiful blue crabs, oysters, and clams fueled a prosperous seafood industry, but pollution has sharply reduced shellfish harvests. From 1975 to 1981, officials banned all commercial fishing in the river, in order for its waters and wildlife to recover following leakage of the pesticide Kepone from a manufacturer in Hopewell.

FOLLOWING PAGES: HAMPTON ROADS, VIRGINIA

Coral-pink sunset highlights the U.S.S. Coral Sea, one of many warships to frequent Hampton Roads, a broad estuary at the mouth of the James River. Home to Norfolk Naval Base—the world's largest—and to the Newport News shipyard, Hampton Roads has witnessed an endless procession of ships bound for innumerable wars. It was here that the Civil War ironclads, Merrimack and Monitor, predecessors of all modern ships of war, staged their historic duel in 1862.

■ THE WATERS OF THE Mississippi and Missouri Rivers and the Rio Grande empty into the Gulf of Mexico south of New Orleans and near Brownsville, Texas, respectively—just a bit more than 500 miles apart, as the gull flies. This simple detail of geography can lead to all sorts of fancies, if you're so inclined, for the relative proximity of their mouths matches not at all the vast range of the terrain encompassed by America's three great heartland rivers.

It's fun to imagine, as you walk along a Galveston beach, that your toes are bathed simultaneously in the spring thaw of Rocky Mountain glaciers, seepage from desert springs in Texas, runoff from Great Plains thunderstorms, and snowmelt from Minnesota's North Woods. Trout swam in these waters, moose and mountain lions and pronghorn drank from them, and alligators basked in them, all before Gulf currents swirled them together into the warm waves that now lap these sands.

The historical legacy of these rivers is as broad and diverse as their landscapes. The Mississippi's name derives from Native American words meaning simply "big river," and that ancient description suits it well. It can be a mile-and-a-half wide or more as it rolls through the Louisiana bayou country, carrying in its broad brown flow waters from more than 40 percent of the continental United States. In the centuries since Spain, England, France, and then the new United States struggled to control North America, the river has served as a vital highway for explorers, a field of battle in war, and a lifeline in commerce.

THE GULF

■ MEL WHITE ■

Nominally a tributary, the Missouri rivals the Mississippi both physically and historically, and is in fact the longer of the two. (Together, they comprise the fourth-longest river system in the world.) The Missouri provided a pathway west for Lewis and Clark on their epic journey of discovery, and after them came fur traders, merchants, and settlers as America sought its Manifest Destiny. Just as steamboats plied the Mississippi's waters, they eventually navigated the Missouri, ascending all the way to Fort Benton, Montana, where the foothills of the Rocky Mountains define the horizon of the Great Plains.

Steamboats once cruised the lower stretches of the Rio Grande, too, though this river never became a major transportation route. The Rio Grande has been a different sort of lifeline: a long, narrow oasis in the midst of parched terrain. Indians of the Pueblo Culture, in what is now New Mexico, used its waters to irrigate crops, and today the Rio Grande remains critical to agriculture and other human needs along much of its course to the Gulf. In the lower Rio Grande Valley, booming human population and intensive agriculture have allocated every cubic foot of the river's flow for one use or another, from grapefruit groves to wildlife habitat.

The Mississippi, the Missouri, and the Rio Grande—their waters blend in the Gulf, but they're as different as bald cypress, prairie grass, and cactus, or blues, cowboy songs, and Tejano tunes. Each is indisputably one of America's great rivers, and each repays modern-day exploration with rewards as varied as the lands they traverse.

LOWER MISSISSIPPI RIVER   *Lights aglow under a rising moon, the* Mississippi Que

ns upstream from New Orleans, recalling the gloried age of steamboats, Mark Twain, and King Cotton.

MISSISSIPPI

STERNWHEELER—LOUISIANA

■ THE MISSISSIPPI IS BORN at Lake Itasca, amid the boreal forests and marshy bogs of northern Minnesota. Generations of travelers have photographed each other at the lake's tiny outlet stream; crossing the Mississippi in a single stride makes a classic summer vacation snapshot.

But an argument could be made that the real Mississippi—the mighty Mississippi of steamboats and barges, the midcontinent's dynamic business artery—begins downstream at St. Anthony Falls, in the Twin Cities of Minneapolis and St. Paul. Here, the only waterfall on the entire river marked the limit of navigation when the first steamboat arrived in 1823. It's still the end of the line for today's big barge tows, which depart laden with Midwestern wheat and other commodities. Over the years the falls have been reshaped and tamed by dams, but they remain an evocative symbol, for it was the water power they provided to local lumber and grain mills that helped build Minneapolis.

It doesn't take long, on a visit to the Twin Cities, to see that local folks prize their stretch of the Mississippi beyond its historical importance as a trade route. Attractive developments line its banks both upstream and down from St. Anthony Falls, featuring shops and restaurants popular with tourists and residents alike. And it's heartening to see that conservationists have worked to save green space amid the glitter of commerce, developing parks and trails on both banks of the river.

Efforts to preserve the river's natural qualities were aided in 1988 by the creation of the Mississippi National River and Recreation Area, an innovative National Park Service project. Though the federal agency owns less than 50 acres of land itself, it coordinates development along 72 miles of the Mississippi, working in partnership with state and local governments and private enterprise to enhance natural and historical resources. Perhaps the most enjoyable place to appreciate the rewards of all this effort is in the Mississippi Gorge Regional Park. In a canoe or along a trail here—just a figurative stone's throw from downtown skyscrapers and the international airport—tree-covered bluffs create a corridor of beauty and comparative peace along a watery highway busy with commercial barges.

Heading south from Minnesota, through Iowa and into the rolling farmland of northeastern Missouri, I stopped at a riverside town where the economy runs not on barge traffic but on memories. It was a clear but chilly weekday in Hannibal, and so I could only imagine the summer crowds of literary pilgrims who arrive to walk streets once roamed by a mischievous boy named Sam Clemens. As the writer Mark Twain, Hannibal's most famous native son has come to embody the romantic spirit of the Mississippi River for millions of people around the world.

Looking over the shops, diners, motels, and assorted tourist clutter called Tom Sawyer This or Becky Thatcher That, I couldn't help thinking that it would take the author of the *Adventures of Huckleberry Finn* himself to do comic and ironic justice to all the uses and abuses of his life and art. Despite the veneer of tourism, it was a thrill for this true fan to see the house the Clemens family moved into in 1843, when Sam was seven years old: The upstairs rear bedroom that was the model for Tom Sawyer's room, the simple kitchen, the parlor where John Clemens (the inspiration for Judge Thatcher in *The Adventures of Tom Sawyer*) met legal clients, and where he no doubt felt the need at times to reprimand his high-spirited son.

A few blocks east, the Mississippi River—where "in summer time we used to borrow skiffs whose owners were not present and go down the river," Twain later wrote—glides past at the foot of Cardiff Hill. Here on the riverbank, young Sam watched riverboats come and go, and decided early on that the life of a steamboat pilot was the grandest in the world.

In 1857 he apprenticed as a river pilot, gaining his pilot's license two years later. As Mark Twain, he put his experiences into a memoir called *Life on the Mississippi*, assuredly one of the great river books of all time. For more than a century, readers have felt themselves in the wheelhouse with Twain as he colorfully describes the glamour, excitement, and danger of steamboat travel, and the prodigious skill and memory required to be a pilot on the constantly mutating river.

I saw something of what the old-time steamboats faced when, continuing downstream, I visited Memphis, Tennessee's Mud Island Park, a recreational complex on a downtown island just a few blocks from historic Beale Street. Here the River Walk, a scaled-down replica of the Mississippi, condenses the river's lower 1,000 miles into less than a half-mile of intricately shaped concrete, steel, and slate, reproducing every meander and convolution from Cairo, Illinois, to New Orleans. As I strode along at a mile per step, I tried to imagine committing to memory all the river's bends and islands, knowing that the safety of passengers and cargo depended on the ability to navigate around every hazard even on foggy, moonless nights. I could only think that, for Mark Twain, writing novels must have been positively relaxing by comparison.

Like many other cities, Memphis for years turned its back on the river that made it prosperous. Mud Island—once a neglected wasteland, now a lively focal point for downtown fun—is a graphic symbol of how that attitude has changed. A monorail shuttles visitors from the mainland over a narrow channel of the river to a visitor center on the landscaped island, where the River Walk, a concert pavilion, and the *Memphis Belle* B-17 bomber from World War II are among the attractions. And for those who'd like a taste of Mark Twain's era, there's a museum dedicated to the Mississippi, complete with a full-size model of an old-time steamboat.

It took me four minutes to stroll from Memphis to Vicksburg along the Mud Island River Walk. (I could have done it in less time but, tempted by sunset, I lingered awhile at an overlook squinting at the fiery orange ball that hovered above the Arkansas bottomlands.) By car, the real trip takes four hours or so, and somewhere along the way—though no one knows exactly where—you will cross one of the most historic routes in the early exploration of America.

EXPLORING THE MISSISSIPPI — 1541

First Europeans to see and cross the Mississippi, Hernando de Soto and his band confront riverside chieftains in this fanciful depiction. "Secure the passage or die," he told his men.

In 1541, while making his ruthless — murderous might be more accurate—way across the South, the Spaniard Hernando de Soto and the members of his expedition arrived at the great river they had been hearing about from Indians, when they weren't too busy burning and butchering to listen. Somewhere between today's Memphis and Vicksburg, they became the first Europeans to see the Mississippi, and they were suitably impressed. "Many of these conquerors said this river was larger than the Danube," one of de Soto's chroniclers wrote; another observed that "if a man stood still on the other side one could not tell whether he were a man or something else."

De Soto crossed the Mississippi and wandered for nearly a year in search of a "rich country" where Indians went about wearing golden hats. His efforts proved totally futile. When the expedition returned to the river in 1542, its leader caught a fever and died, and his body was sunk in its waters. His companions were the first to record the experience of the Mississippi in spring flood. "And it was a most magnificent spectacle to behold," one wrote. "That which previously had been forests and fields was converted now into a sea, for from each bank the water extended across more than twenty leagues of terrain…and nothing was visible except the pine needles and branches of the highest trees."

It was the threat of just such catastrophic floods that caused many cities along the Mississippi—Memphis and Vicksburg among them—to be built on bluffs, safely above those periodic inland seas. During the Civil War, Vicksburg's location gave it such a strong defensive capability that it was nicknamed the "Gibraltar of America." Union forces tried unsuccessfully to take it several times from the river before Gen. Ulysses S. Grant attacked from land, capturing the city on July 4, 1863, after a 47-day siege.

In Vicksburg, I stopped to tour the national military park, and to visit the national cemetery where white monuments stand row after row on a hill above the Mississippi. At a Confederate battery position called Fort Hill, I looked down on a landscape much changed from those Civil War days, one that displays graphic evidence of the river's power.

In 1876, Mississippi floodwaters altered the river's course literally overnight, cutting across a narrow neck of land and leaving Vicksburg on a slowly silting-in backwater. What had been a thriving river city began to die, like a limb that had lost its blood

VICKSBURG CAMPAIGN — 1863

Union fleet challenges Confederate artillery esconced on the bluffs of Vicksburg in April of 1863. A 47-day siege of the city followed, culminating in the fall of this "Gibraltar of America."

supply. In 1903, the Army Corps of Engineers diverted the nearby Yazoo River into the old channel of the Mississippi, a feat of reconstructive surgery that restored Vicksburg's port status and kept its name alive as more than a historic memory.

Study a map and you'll see innumerable spots where state lines no longer coincide with the Mississippi's course—evidence of this river's ever-shifting channel. These squiggles are trivialities, however, compared to some historic wanderings. Once, the Ohio River flowed down the modern Mississippi's midsection, while the Mississippi ran on a parallel course to the west, about where the White River now crosses Arkansas. Between them lay a long, thin strip of high ground that still stands today as Crowley's Ridge, the only wrinkle in the flat tablecloth of the eastern Arkansas landscape. Vegetation on this ridge is more like that of the Appalachians than of the rest of Arkansas. Nowhere else do tulip trees grow naturally west of the Mississippi; but that's because just 20,000 years ago—only yesterday in geologic terms— Crowley's Ridge was *east* of the Mississippi.

Along the south section of the Mississippi, in the level terrain of the Gulf Coastal Plain—the land of bayous and oxbow lakes, bald cypress and water tupelo, alligators and egrets—the river doesn't need much encouragement to change course. Geologists believe that over the past 6,000 years the Mississippi has had at least five different outlets to the Gulf of Mexico. This fact is by no means limited to abstract scientific interest; without long-standing and continuing efforts to contain it, the Mississippi would have broken through its west bank upstream from Baton Rouge sometime in the past three or four decades, and begun pouring its waters down the Atchafalaya River channel. Had that happened, New Orleans, the country's second-largest port, would have been reduced to backwater status, just as Vicksburg was more than a century ago.

Sitting in the Café du Monde in the French Quarter, eating a beignet and listening to a street saxophonist play the theme from *Sesame Street*, I had a hard time thinking of such a distressing possibility. Just so, I preferred not to contemplate how only an elaborate system of levees, dating from the 18th century, keeps much of this aristocratic, gaudy, historic old city from lying under six or more feet of water.

I ambled over to the Moon Walk, the riverside promenade at the edge of the French Quarter, and watched a cargo ship steaming down toward Head of Passes, the spot in the river delta that marks mile zero for Mississippi navigation. Out there in the Gulf, the Mississippi has come more than 2,300 miles from little Lake Itasca in Minnesota, having united waters from the Appalachians and the Rockies, the North Woods and the Great Plains. I thought of the words of Mark Twain, who when he heard in 1882 of new efforts to limit Mississippi flooding wrote that "ten thousand River Commissions... cannot tame that lawless stream, cannot curb it or confine it ...."

I thought, too, of my earlier stroll along the model of the Mississippi at Memphis's Mud Island. When I had reached the sidewalk grid representing New Orleans, I found the entire city drowned as if by a monstrous flood. It was no gloomy omen, though, only spray from a fountain splashed across the walk by a gusty wind playing at being a hurricane. ■

RIVER WALK — MEMPHIS, TENNESSEE

Reducing the mighty Mississippi to human proportions, the River Walk draws visitors to Mud Island Park in Memphis with a scale-model reproduction of the river and its surroundings, complete with miniaturized topography, cities, bridges, and oxbow lakes.

NORTH CENTRAL MINNESOTA *Shaking hands with the Mississippi's traditional headwaters, a you*

ke Itasca, a popular northern Minnesota tourist site whose name stems from the Latin phrase *veritas caput*, or true head.

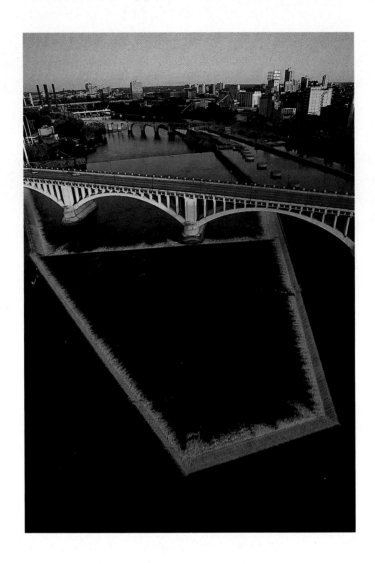

ST. ANTHONY FALLS — MINNESOTA

Tamed by dynamite and reshaped by concrete, St. Anthony Falls (above) follows man-made symmetry today as it divides Minneapolis (right) from St. Paul. The only waterfall to occur on the Mississippi, this cascade originally blocked steamboats from continuing farther upriver. Water power provided by the falls turned the wheels of the lumber and grain mills that laid the foundation for today's Twin Cities.

PIKES PEAK STATE PARK — IOWA

Encased in crystal by winter ice, native grasses of Pikes Peak State Park in northeastern Iowa overlook wooded islands amid the partially frozen Mississippi (opposite). Here the river flows through a section of Upper Mississippi River National Wildlife and Fish Refuge, which extends through four states and provides sustenance for migrant swans, geese, and ducks, as well as nesting bald eagles.

ARCHES OLD AND NEW — ST. LOUIS, MISSOURI *Dwarfed by perspective, the city's trade*

…ay Arch nestles beneath the graceful lattice of Eads Bridge, the world's first major steel span, completed in 1874.

TOM SAWYER DAYS—
HANNIBAL, MISSOURI

Numbered paper plates stuck to their backs, contestants vie in a fence-painting competition (opposite) that honors Hannibal's most famous native son, Samuel L. Clemens (better known as Mark Twain). Inspired by an episode in The Adventures of Tom Sawyer, *the contest highlights an annual festival.*

GRACELAND—
MEMPHIS, TENNESSEE

From rockabilly rebel to Vegas crooner, the many faces of Elvis crowd the walls of Graceland— the King's enduring castle, transformed into a Memphis tourist magnet.

NEW ORLEANS, LOUISIANA *In tune with tradition, the Preservation Hall Jazz Band (above) continues to cel*
that uniquely American musical style that first took shape in the clubs of New Orleans and its French Quarter: Dixieland.

FOLLOWING PAGES: LAND'S END — GULF OF MEXICO *Land and sea converge in the ever-changing Mississippi Delta, as the river — now more than 2,300 miles from its northern Minnesota source — at last reaches the Gulf.*

MISSOURI

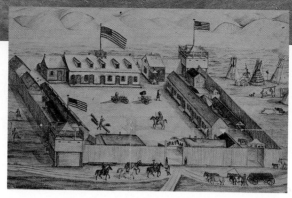

FORT PIERRE, SOUTH DAKOTA—1855

■ THOMAS JEFFERSON stands forthrightly at the entrance of St. Louis's Museum of Westward Expansion, offering a perpetual welcome to visitors under the gleaming and graceful Gateway Arch. Outside, just a musket shot away, flows the Mississippi— an impressive sight but the wrong river. This museum is all about the growth of the young United States following Jefferson's momentous Louisiana Purchase of 1803, and the river inextricably linked with the exploration and settlement of that vast territory is, of course, the Missouri.

Not getting its due is nothing unusual for the Big Muddy. As historians have often pointed out, the Missouri logically should have been considered the major river that flows to the Gulf of Mexico, while the upper Mississippi should have been relegated to tributary status. The Missouri is far longer, measuring upstream from the rivers' confluence just north of St. Louis, and at that point its flow averages a bit greater than the Mississippi's. History didn't favor the Missouri that way, of course, but as a central element in our country's development, its role is unsurpassed.

As I traveled up the lower Missouri, I was paralleling the route followed by thousands of pioneers heading west in the middle and late 19th century. Taking steamboats upriver, they disembarked at Independence, Missouri, and outfitted themselves with wagons, oxen, horses, and supplies for the long trek along the Oregon Trail or other trails that led to California, seeking their promised lands.

I stopped in historic Independence to revisit one of my favorite museums, just south of downtown. The National Frontier Trails Center chronicles the pioneer era in exhibits that vividly recount the hope and heartbreak of those who undertook the journey. I enjoyed the dioramas and displays of artifacts, but was especially drawn to excerpts from the letters and diaries of travelers. "I am determined to go, and I cannot think of anything which would turn me back," an 1846 immigrant wrote, showing the spirit that compelled so many to undertake the trip west. "We are all glad that we are going to have a home somewhere at last," another wrote from California in 1850, relieved that her long ordeal was nearly ended.

In nearby Kansas City, another collection recalls the steamboat era. The Arabia Steamboat Museum, less than a half-mile from the river, displays many of the goods carried by *Arabia*, a 171-foot-long boat that struck a submerged tree trunk and slowly sank in 1856 at Quindaro Bend, in what is now Kansas. The shifting river buried *Arabia* in mud, preserving its 200 tons of cargo—intended for general stores upriver—in astonishingly pristine condition. Exhumed in 1988, the ship's relics offer an absorbing look at mid-19th-century life: thousands of shoes and boots, porcelain buttons and bottled cherries from France, barrels of spiced pigs' feet, bolts of silk from Asia, Baltimore oysters, whale-oil lamps, thimbles, South American coffee beans, nails and doorknobs, hand-blown glass beads from Bohemia. I wandered through the museum halls transfixed until closing time. Gawking at this time capsule is a relatively guilt-free experience, too, because *Arabia* sank so leisurely that no lives were lost save for one poor mule that had been tied to equipment on deck.

Pioneers and steamboats played major roles in the pageant of the Missouri River, but it's impossible to think of this waterway without considering its part in one of America's greatest adventure tales, the expedition of Meriwether Lewis and William Clark and their Corps of Discovery. President Thomas Jefferson charged them with the task of exploring the newly purchased Louisiana Territory and finding a route to the Pacific Northwest. Lewis and Clark set out from near St. Louis in May of 1804, and by the time they returned to a hero's welcome in September of 1806, they had filled in a vital part of the map of North America and blazed a trail through history—a trail that in large part followed the Missouri.

My own Missouri River journey next took me upstream, through the rolling prairie of the Great Plains, to the North Dakota Lewis and Clark Interpretive Center in Washburn. Sited on a broad curve of the Missouri, this airy and attractive museum is full of well-designed exhibits and artifacts of the historic expedition, including journal excerpts that demonstrate spelling as eccentric as the descriptions are evocative. The sandbars and cottonwoods outside no doubt look much the same as they did when the Corps of Discovery spent the winter of 1804-05 near here on its way west, though the meandering river has altered its channel over the intervening two centuries.

A short distance upstream stands a reconstruction of Lewis and Clark's winter quarters, which they called Fort Mandan. The original had burned by the time the expedition returned in 1806, and no one knows exactly where it stood. As I walked toward the triangular fort, built of tall cottonwood palings, I was greeted, appropriately enough, by the deep, resounding crack of a muzzle-loading rifle. A group of black-powder buffs was holding a competitive shoot at the fort; several of them were camped nearby in tepees, wearing fringed buckskin jackets and other old-time garb. It added a bit of atmosphere to the morning, though their targets weren't elk or deer but circles on paper.

Things were quieter on a trail a few miles upstream, at Knife River Indian Villages National Historic Site, where the loudest sound I heard was the sweetly bubbling song of a bobolink fluttering over the prairie. On a small bluff overlooking the Knife River just above its confluence with the Missouri, my path crossed a grassy field dotted with circular depressions up to 40 feet wide, like huge dimples in the green earth.

Two centuries ago, this spot was a bustling community of dome-shaped earthen lodges, alive with the cries of children playing and the songs of women and girls tending riverside crops of corn, beans, and squash. Three Hidatsa villages stood here then, an association of linked towns whose total population Lewis and Clark estimated at around 5,000—roughly one-third that of Washington, D.C. at the time. As curious about the Corps of Discovery as its members were about them, the Indians welcomed and traded with the explorers during their winter sojourn here, helping them survive bitterly cold weather during which Clark wrote, "last night was excessively Cold the Murckery this morning Stood at 40° below 0...."

MISSOURI RIVER FUR TRADERS

Though traders and Indians sometimes fought—as depicted here—lucrative bartering often prevailed, spurring white exploration of the lands of the Louisiana Purchase.

Passing among the lodge sites, my boots retraced (figuratively, at least) the marks of some very famous moccasins. Sacagawea (sometimes spelled Sacajawea), the Shoshone woman who accompanied Lewis and Clark and became an honored legend of the American West, once lived in this very village. Kidnapped as a child, she had been taken into the Hidatsa tribe and was the common-law wife of Toussaint Charbonneau, who lived with the Hidatsa and served the expedition as translator.

Change came quickly to the Missouri River region in the wake of Lewis and Clark, as fur traders began to exploit its rich resources. Worldwide demand for beaver hats fueled new explorations into the Rocky Mountains, as well as the construction of trading posts along the Missouri where trappers, Indians, and merchants mingled.

Regional center of the fur trade was Fort Union, built in 1828 at the confluence of the Missouri and Yellowstone Rivers, astride what is now the Montana-North Dakota border. Here Kenneth McKenzie, manager for John Jacob Astor's American Fur

Company, ruled with such authority that he was called "the king of the Missouri." Artist and naturalist John James Audubon, painter George Catlin, and other notables visited Fort Union over the years. Rough-hewn at first, the fort grew more refined over time, as reflected in today's beautifully reconstructed "Bourgeois House," or manager's residence, complete with white picket fence, dormers, and neatly shuttered windows.

Continuing upriver into central Montana, I stopped one beautiful fall day at one of the most famous places on Lewis and Clark's route, Decision Point, at the confluence of the Marias and Missouri Rivers. Here I stood on a small hill and looked down on the two streams, just as the explorers did when they were trying to determine which was the main channel. After nine days of reconnoitering, the two leaders chose the southern river, going against the collective opinion of the rest of their company.

The explorers had learned from Indians that they would find a series of waterfalls on the "real" Missouri: Having gone ahead of the rest of the party, Meriwether Lewis soon confirmed they were on the right course when he saw the Great Falls, which he called "the grandest sight I ever beheld." A series of five such waterfalls within twelve miles created one of the journey's most difficult passages: a three-week portage during which the Corps laboriously dragged its boats overland. Clark wrote of the effort that "the fatigue which we have to encounter is incretiatable."

The Great Falls still exist, in and near the city of the same name, though they're strangled by hydroelectric dams just upstream that divert

MANDAN VILLAGE LIFE

Mandan women negotiate the Missouri River in bullboats made of buffalo hides stretched over willow frames. Above them rise the circular earthen lodges of their blufftop village.

the Missouri's flow into side channels. Imagination can help modern visitors here conjure a notion of what the falls looked like before those massive concrete arcs were put in place, but it's still a poor substitute for what Lewis called the "whitest beaten froath" and "billows of great hight."

West of Great Falls, the Missouri leaves the vast spaces of Big Sky Country for the Rockies, as wrinkled and dun-colored hills dotted with ponderosa pines begin to rise beside the river. The Corps passed through one rock-walled strait of such drama that Lewis named it "the gates of the rocky mountains"; today a canyon called the Gates of the Mountains is a popular destination for tour boats, which cruise beneath cliffs soaring more than 1,000 feet above them. Here and for many miles upstream, dams and reservoirs have transformed the river, but above Townsend it runs as freely through its broad valleys as it did when Lewis and Clark arrived in July 1805. Within days, the Corps would reach the place where the Missouri begins.

Begins officially, that is. In a flat plain bordered by low hills, the expedition found a spot where three meandering rivers met. Unwilling to designate one as the Missouri, Lewis and Clark named them for the President and the Secretaries of State and Treasury. Hence, though the waters of the Missouri actually originate in the snowmelt of the Rockies far beyond, the river officially starts here, at the confluence of three small streams called the Jefferson, the Madison, and the Gallatin.

At Missouri Headwaters State Park, in Montana, I stood on a limestone outcrop as the explorers once did, looking down at three rivers of notable similarity. Their beds are formed, wrote Lewis, "of smooth pebble and gravel," and none seems significantly larger than the others. Here again, the party faced a decision: Which fork would lead most directly to the Pacific?

They followed the Jefferson, and so did I for a few miles, wanting to see a bit of one of the progenitors of the great river I had experienced in full maturity more than 2,300 miles away. At Three Forks, Clark wrote that a hunting party had seen "great numbers of antelopes" nearby. By chance I also saw more than 50 pronghorn, loafing in an alfalfa field. I also spotted two golden eagles, a prairie falcon, a mule deer, and two bald eagles, all species familiar to Lewis and Clark. And perched in a pine beside the Jefferson was a jay-like Clark's nutcracker, one of many species discovered during the expedition, and one that today bears the co-leader's name.

I got out of my car and, as I walked toward the river, almost stepped on a four-foot bull snake. It's a species that can be aggressive at times, but this fellow was sluggish and passive in the chill of a fall morning. Down by the water the cottonwoods were turning bright yellow, making a striking and beautiful contrast with the dark green of the conifers farther up the slopes. Snow was predicted for high elevations that evening.

Here, Lewis and Clark began the most difficult and dangerous part of their journey. Clark wrote of the mountain crossing that "all appear perfectly to have made up their minds to Succeed in the expedition or perish in the attempt." Looking upriver, I thought of the daunting snows and cliffs that lay ahead along the Continental Divide. I zipped up my jacket, headed back to the car, and turned the heater up a notch. ∎

CANYON FERRY LAKE — MONTANA

Nearly incandescent against the prairie's blue sky, sunflowers bask beside the dammed waters of the upper Missouri's Canyon Ferry Lake, near Townsend, Montana.

THREE FORKS — MONTANA *Convoluted confluence of the Jefferson (left) a.*

...dison Rivers marks the official beginning of the Missouri; the Gallatin joins in seven miles downstream.

GREAT FALLS — MONTANA

"The grandest sight I ever beheld," wrote Meriwether Lewis of the Great Falls of the Missouri, noting "a roaring too tremendious to be mistaken" and five separate cataracts over a twelve-mile stretch. Today, the man-made buttress of Ryan Dam-tames the river, though its waters still plummet down a portion of their natural course, while hawks (above, left) continue to patrol.

WHITE CLIFFS — MONTANA   *Shaped by wind and water, mushroom-shaped hoodoos spr*

the White Cliffs, which mark a wild and scenic section of the upper Missouri just downstream from Fort Benton.

FORT PECK DAM — MONTANA

*One of the largest public-works projects of the 1930s,
eastern Montana's massive Fort Peck Dam backs up the Missouri for about a
hundred miles. The resulting reservoir boasts a shoreline longer than California's—
more than 1,500 miles—and dimensions so grand that windstorms
here can kick up ocean-magnitude waves.*

WHEAT FIELD—NORTH DAKOTA

Rising winds, gathering gloom, and a lightning strike signal an approaching storm for this field of wheat in central North Dakota, not far from the Missouri (below). Today, the river's fertile bottomlands help sustain the immensely productive northern plains, where wheat, corn, oats, soybeans, and cattle have largely displaced the original prairie and its herds of bison, elk, and deer.

FOLLOWING PAGES: SQUAW CREEK—MISSOURI

Reminiscent of an earlier day, waterfowl throng lake and sky at Squaw Creek National Wildlife Refuge, in northwestern Missouri. Lewis and Clark reported great numbers of "Geese, ducks of dift. kinds, & a fiew Swan" all along their journey up the Missouri River, and areas such as Squaw Creek continue to offer visitors at least an echo of what the explorers saw.

RIO GRANDE

TAOS PUEBLO — NEW MEXICO

■ "FORWARD PADDLE! Back paddle hard two strokes!" Our guide called out her commands expertly, and three other rafters and I did our inexpert best to execute them as we slid past huge boulders of volcanic basalt and over foaming falls on a stretch of the upper Rio Grande known as "the Racecourse," about 20 miles southwest of Taos, New Mexico. None of us had much rafting knowledge, but we dug our paddles into the churning water, pulled for all we were worth, and shot through the rapids one after another without mishap—a triumph of enthusiasm over inexperience, perhaps. Every now and then, after an intricate bit of maneuvering, we raised our paddles and touched the blades together over the raft: a wooden "high five" celebrating a good run.

It was a near-perfect late-September day; the air was crisp, the sun was warm, a breeze stirred the riverside junipers, and the cloudless sky was bluer than the feathers of the kingfisher that flew past as we relaxed and let the current carry us. The sparkling drops of cool water that splashed up as we scudded along felt good on my skin, and in the calm stretches between rapids I leaned back against the raft and watched the gorge pass, the slopes of the tall cliffs dotted with juniper, sagebrush, and the yellow-flowering shrub called chamiza.

One component of a designated wild and scenic section of the river, the Race-course remains a popular rafting run, more open than a stretch just upstream known as the Taos Box, where cliffs rise almost straight up to heights of 800 feet or more, creating a chasm of awesome verticality. Seen from the air, this part of the upper Rio Grande seems a ragged scar across the flat scrubland. Its course is determined wholly by geology; the juncture of two slowly separating tectonic plates determines the direction of this canyon, while erosive waters derived in part from the snows of the Colorado Rockies continually shape and polish the stone.

At La Junta Point, a spectacular spot 18 miles north of Taos, the Red River joins the Rio Grande and proffers more evidence of the river's ancient past. Canyon walls show layers of basalt—deposited by long-extinct volcanoes—alternating with rock formed from gravels washed down from surrounding mountains. Tall pinnacles and palisades, the patient handiwork of ages, loom over the river. Just such natural beauty helped the upper Rio Grande win designation as one of America's first wild and scenic rivers, in 1968. Today, thousands of visitors a year enjoy both the scenery and the white-water, in places far more challenging than the intermediate-level rapids I experienced along the Racecourse.

When a devastating drought struck this region some time around the 13th century, the Rio Grande provided more than recreation: Its waters meant survival in a parched land. Indians who had lived to the west and northwest abandoned their cliff dwellings and moved here, building adobe structures near the river and creating what came to be called the Pueblo Culture. It was these peoples whom the Spanish conquistador Francisco Vasquez de Coronado encountered in 1540, as he traveled the Southwest in his single-minded quest for gold. He was the first in a procession of explorers and colonizers drawn from the Old World and, later, the infant United States. The intervening centuries have seen conflict and compromise among Native American, Spanish, and Anglo societies in the upper Rio Grande region—first the literal conflict of war and revolution, then the mutual concessions that go into building a multicultural community. But Pueblo society endures to this day, in villages scattered along the Rio Grande south of Albuquerque to Taos.

Late one afternoon I visited Coronado State Monument, which preserves the site of Kuaua, an ancient Rio Grande pueblo near Bernalillo, New Mexico. The town was abandoned near the start of the 17th century, and what I saw was a partial reconstruction of its adobe walls. Displayed in a museum room, though, were original murals removed from the village kiva, or underground ceremonial room, in a 1935 archaeological investigation. In one painting a man played a hoop-and-stick game, possibly a ritual to bring rain; in another, a lively jackrabbit had imprints of human hands superimposed on one hind foot, perhaps symbolizing a hunt. Ghostly figures in faded black, red, white, and yellow evoked the people who once lived here, who planted corn and beans along the river, and who watched as strange men appeared one day wearing armor, mounted on horses.

In September of 1540, a Coronado lieutenant named Pedro de Castañeda arrived near this spot and wrote of "a province of twelve pueblos, on the banks of a large and mighty river.... To the east there is a snow-covered sierra, very high and rough." A similar scene greeted me, as a gusty south wind blew puffy white clouds over Sandia Mountain, Castañeda's "sierra." The slanting sun made the peak appear rough indeed, its pointed spires, jagged outcrops, and dissected ridgelines lit in stark relief. At the end of a dry summer, though, the Rio Grande seemed not so large and mighty, flowing placidly under cottonwoods and willows.

From an airplane or a high overlook, the Rio Grande's streamside vegetation plainly marks it as a green thread of life in an arid landscape, an oasis today as it was for the early Pueblo peoples. From this point down, cities that grew up along its banks dot the river at irregular intervals: Albuquerque, Las Cruces, El Paso and Juárez, Del Rio, Laredo and Nuevo Laredo, and Brownsville. At El Paso—from the early Spaniards' El Paso del Norte, the place where the river cut a pass through the mountains, thus creating a gateway from Old Mexico to New—the Rio Grande becomes an international boundary. All along this Texas-Mexico border the Hispanic culture dominates; Spanish is heard more commonly than English in shops and on the street.

My favorite spot along the river has nothing to do with cities or human societies, though. It is instead one of the wildest and most beautiful places in all of North America: Big Bend National Park, which encompasses more than 800,000 acres where the Rio Grande makes a "big bend" northward on its generally southeasterly path to the Gulf of Mexico.

FRONTIER JUSTICE—TEXAS 1880s

The legendary "Law West of the Pecos," Judge Roy Bean ran a lively courtroom in his saloon in Langtry, Texas, just north of the Rio Grande. He routinely relied on a law book, revolver, and handcuffs to serve up 1880s justice across a region as wild as it was remote. Some offenders brought before Bean were ordered to buy drinks for the jury that convicted them.

I offer the caveat here that not every traveler may be as enthusiastic as I about Big Bend. Most of its huge expanse is Chihuahuan Desert, its beauty the type usually described as stark or harsh. Maybe it's because I come from a land of ubiquitous greenery and humidity that I value my visits here so much. I love the open space, the agave and cactus, the weird and wonderful rock formations created by volcanoes, ancient seas, uplift, and erosion. I love hiking in the Chisos Mountains, which rise like a cool, verdant island from the dry desert floor.

At Big Bend, the Rio Grande again becomes officially wild and scenic. Its carved canyons outdo in scale and grandeur even those of the Taos Box. Like liquid sandpaper, the sediment-laden river here continues to erode its way down as it has for millennia, while the surrounding land has slowly risen. The result is three canyons—Santa Elena, Mariscal, and Boquillas—where in places sheer rock cliffs rise as much as 1,500 feet, creating a scene as claustrophobically constricted as a city street lined with skyscrapers. Outfitters offer raft trips, and at Santa Elena you can wade across Terlingua Creek and hike into the canyon. The trail is fairly short and easy, yet it penetrates far enough into the chasm to provide a taste of magnificent isolation.

If you're lucky enough to be alone in Santa Elena (dawn is best), you can create all sorts of fantasies of primeval wildness, as the haunting songs of canyon wrens echo from the cliffs. Bones of the largest flying animal ever found on Earth, a pterodactyl with a 36-foot wingspan, were found in Big Bend in 1971, and if that doesn't spark your imagination, nothing will. One of my favorite Big Bend experiences took place as I lay on a rock in the canyon one May morning—and saw a golden eagle soar lazily in the narrow slit of sky high above. No dinosaur, but still an inspiring sight.

The Rio Grande's role as linear oasis is as evident at Big Bend as it is anywhere along its course. A few hundred yards from the river, desert plants such as creosotebush, ocotillo, and cholla grow; near the water, cottonwood, willow, buttonbush, and reeds thrive, while beaver, herons, ducks, and shorebirds feed and rest. Most of the water that makes such un-deserty life possible comes not from the upper Rio Grande but from the Rio Conchos, which flows into the Rio Grande from Mexico about 50 miles upstream from the park. Between El Paso and Rio Conchos, irrigation and other human uses so reduce the Rio Grande's flow that at times it's little more than a trickle.

The Rio Grande runs free through Big Bend National Park, but as it approaches the Gulf of Mexico human needs once again impact and increasingly reshape it. The Amistad and Falcon Dams drown miles of riverbed by creating expansive reservoirs. During the river's last 150 or so miles its waters are exploited to a greater extent than anywhere else along its length, both by an enormously fertile agricultural region almost wholly dependent on irrigation canals, and by a fast-growing metropolitan sprawl from McAllen to Brownsville.

In addition to the competing needs of urbanization and farming for the river's limited water, there's another factor in this liquid equation: The lower Rio Grande

Valley ranks among America's most important wildlife habitats. Undervalued and abused for decades, the valley environment and its beleaguered plants and animals are now the focus of serious restoration efforts, some of which require hard decisions about allocation of increasingly overcommitted water resources.

Throughout the 1990s, federal, state, and local governments and private interests have been cooperating to create a wildlife corridor aimed at expanding existing parks and refuges in the valley and linking them to each other, as well as ensuring they get the water they need to be productive. Though its creation has been a long and sometimes controversial process, such a network of preserves should help assure the survival of many rare or localized species, from the tiny buff-bellied hummingbird to the small and secretive ocelot, a spotted cat as elusive as it is beautiful.

Near the end of my Rio Grande journey I visited one of the best of the valley's natural areas, the National Audubon Society's Sabal Palm Grove Sanctuary near Brownsville. Named for a species native to Texas, this preserve is home to the last large stand of such trees left in the United States. Once, 40,000 acres of sabal palms grew in the Rio Grande Valley—prompting Alonso Alvarez de Piñeda, the first European to see the river, to call it *Río de las Palmas*, or River of Palms, in 1519. Today, pretty much all that remains of what he saw north of the river is the sanctuary's 32-acre grove, a lush green bit of the tropics seemingly transplanted north of the border.

Elsewhere in the refuge's 527 acres, staff members plant sabal palms and other native vegetation, trying to expand this small remnant habitat. Their work is made more difficult by upriver dams, which have eliminated annual inundations that in the past brought renewing floodwaters and rich silt to the lower valley. Despite this loss, however, the survival rate of plantings is running more than 80 percent— a hopeful sign for the future. The lower Rio Grande may never again merit the name River of Palms, but if the efforts of conservationists succeed, perhaps its lower valley will continue to be home to ocelots, hook-billed kites, indigo snakes, malachite butterflies, and the countless other species that make up one of America's most diverse natural environments.

The trail at Sabal Palm Sanctuary was quiet the day I visited, save for bird songs and the soft rustling of huge palm fronds in the wind. It was a peaceful place that seemed far from the freeways and malls of Brownsville, the sort of place that refreshes both mind and spirit by recalling earlier times and simpler pleasures. I could only hope that as decisions are made about the Rio Grande's future, the opportunity to experience such wild places—and their beauty—will endure forever. ∎

BANDELIER— NEW MEXICO

Carved grotto and holes that once anchored roof beams mark a cliff face in Frijoles Canyon, Bandelier National Monument, near Santa Fe. Here the Anasazi ancestors of today's Pueblo people once lived, farmed, and hunted, centuries before Columbus.

SIERRA BLANCA — COLORADO *Carrying snowmelt from the lofty San*

Mountains, the upper Rio Grande meanders placidly through southern Colorado's San Luis Valley.

CUMBRES PASS — COLORADO

In a ritual as old as the Old West, cowboys herd cattle through Rio Grande National Forest, working their way from high summer pastures west of Alamosa, Colorado, down through fir and aspen woodlands, to winter grazing areas in the lowlands.

WILD AND SCENIC RIO GRANDE — NEW MEXICO

Looking like colorful water bugs all in a row, rafters lazily string out along a wild and scenic section of the river, in northern New Mexico. Though the Rio Grande flows gently here, its personality can change dramatically: In the famed canyon known as the Taos Box, it rushes through boulder-strewn rapids that offer plenty of thrills for white-water enthusiasts.

BOSQUE DEL APACHE — NEW MEXICO   *Taking wing each dawn to feed in nearby f*

ring sandhill cranes mass by the thousands in Bosque del Apache National Wildlife Refuge, along the Rio Grande.

BIG BEND — TEXAS

Sunrise gilds the walls of Santa Elena Canyon (opposite), in Big Bend National Park,
where silt-laden waters of the Rio Grande have carved numerous chasms through the West Texas
mountains. In 1852, curious explorers launched an empty boat into the mouth of
Santa Elena; only wooden splinters came out the other end. The first successful passage
of this canyon's fearsome rapids took place nearly 50 years later, and now rafting companies routinely
traverse it. Burgeoning blossoms of prickly pear cactus (above), common throughout
Big Bend, echo the warm tones of Santa Elena's cliffs.

FOLLOWING PAGES:
PADRE ISLAND — TEXAS

Sliver of sand amid the blue expanse of Laguna Madre, the southern tip of Padre Island lies
at the end of a causeway connecting this popular beach resort with Port Isabel, on the Texas mainland.
Just south of Port Isabel, the Rio Grande languidly enters the Gulf of Mexico.

■ EVERY RIVER YEARNS FOR THE SEA, but in the arid and mountainous West some never find it. The Humboldt rises amid desert peaks, a good river until it disappears in the alkaline wastes of the Great Basin, a place where rivers go to die. More fortunate streams, born on the better side of a divide, flow freely for a while only to join their destiny with stronger waters, and stronger still, searching, flowing together until they find a river—a great river—with strength and volume to reach journey's end.

There are small coastal rivers that reach the Pacific: the Salinas, Russian, and Klamath; the Rogue and Chehalis. There are powerful inland tributaries that have worked their will upon the land and created history of their own: the Green and San Juan, the Snake and Willamette, the Feather, American, and Stanislaus. But there are only four great rivers that reach the Pacific, gathering precious waters, carving canyons, gorges, and valleys as they force their way to the sea through rugged mountains and ragged uplifted plateaus: the Colorado, the Columbia, the Sacramento, and the San Joaquin.

These rivers offered sustenance and transportation to the native people who lived along them, while alternately teasing and rewarding the Europeans who came to conquer, convert, and trade. Spanish explorers sailed up the Colorado in 1540 on a wild-eyed chase for the golden Cities of Cibola. Yet though their compatriots gazed down at the Grand Canyon, the canyon and the maze it anchors on the Colorado Plateau prevented exploration for over three centuries, until a tough, one-armed Civil War veteran named John Wesley Powell unlocked its mysteries in 1869.

HE PACIFIC

■ PAUL ROBERT WALKER ■

To the north and west, the Sierra Nevada and the vast wetlands of the Sacramento-San Joaquin Delta stymied the Spanish as well. Yet a tributary of the San Joaquin offered American mountain man Jedediah Smith passage over the high sierra in 1827; a dozen years later, a Swiss-born dreamer named John Augustus Sutter sailed through the delta and up the Sacramento into the heart of present-day California.

Still farther north, the awesome power and size of the Columbia at its mouth obscured the river itself, confusing a succession of sea captains looking for the mythical Northwest Passage. Yet once the mouth was discovered, the Columbia brought American and British fur traders into a wilderness of incredible riches; in 1805, it carried Lewis and Clark downriver on the final leg of their great journey to the Pacific. Four decades later, thousands of emigrants, full of dreams and hungry for land, headed west on the Oregon Trail and rafted down the Columbia to the fertile Willamette Valley.

Today, these rivers still fight to reach the sea, but they are low on ammunition. We take their water for cities and farms, for golf courses and swimming pools; we harness their flow for electricity; we divert their channels for convenience. We in the West cannot live without the rivers, but we must ask: Can the rivers live with us? I have traveled along them, following their moods and meanderings, and I know the issues are complex. Yet they must be considered. These are still great rivers, and we must help them with their greatness.

COLUMBIA RIVER SUNSET *Chasing the westering sun, the Columbia seems t*

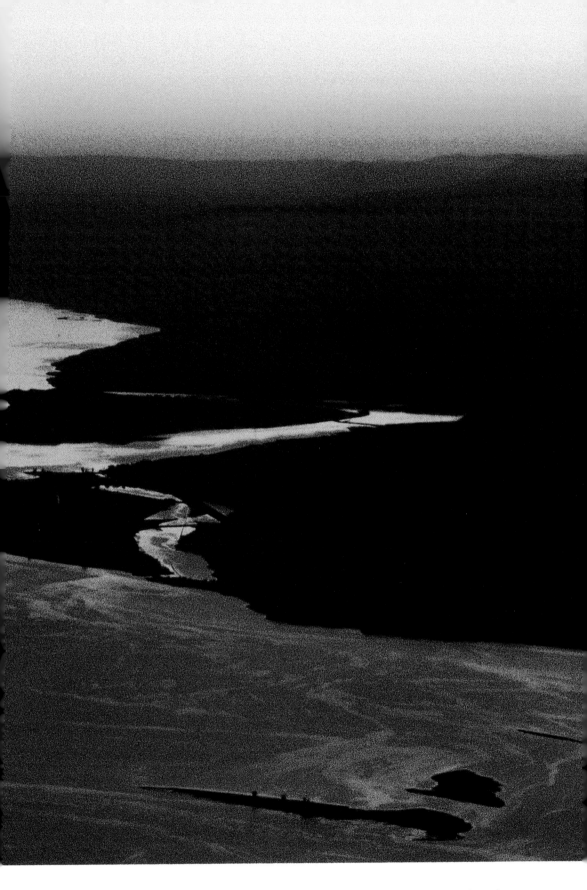

...ard Oregon's distant Mount Hood, establishing the Oregon-Washington border as it rolls on to the broad Pacific.

COLORADO

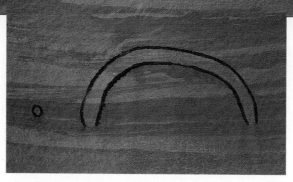

PICTOGRAPH — CANYONLANDS, UTAH

■ THE COLORADO RISES in an alpine meadow in the Rocky Mountains National Park, just west of the Continental Divide. Fed by snowmelt and mountain rains, it rushes down rocky slopes through green-blue forests of pine and spruce, sprinkled with golden aspen. French fur trappers called the upper Colorado *le Grand*, a name that was applied well into the 20th century to that stretch of river upstream from the confluence with the Green. Yet here in the high country on an autumn afternoon, a better name might be *le Petit*. The river seems a fragile thing, perhaps eight feet wide and eight inches deep, bubbling over softly rounded stones, meandering across grassy flats where elk graze peacefully among the trees.

Gazing up at the divide, sharp and forbidding in the fading light of a cloudy day, I see a gash that looks like a road cutting across the slope. But it isn't a road; it's a ditch: the Grand Ditch, built a century ago to capture snowmelt and route it east of the mountains before it could reach the river. This ditch was just the initial assault, for today the Colorado is used and reused like no other river in North America. Every drop of its water is claimed and accounted for, to irrigate farms and ranches, to satisfy thirsty cities, to power lights and air conditioners—serving some 25 million people in what is largely a desert land. Little wonder that in all but the wettest of seasons, the Colorado no longer reaches the sea.

About 16 miles below the divide, Grand Lake sparkles in the morning sun, wispy clouds hanging above its cool blue surface. It is the largest natural lake in the state. A wooden sign on shore declares it "the headwaters of the Colorado," but this is more notion than nature, and Grand Lake has always been a notional place. The Arapaho, who crossed the divide to hunt and fish along its shores, called it Spirit Lake, telling of a great white buffalo that seemed to appear from a hole in the ice during a winter storm.

The Utes, who claimed this land for their own, spoke of a different storm, so wild and powerful that it masked an approaching war party of Arapaho and Cheyenne. As fighting raged along the shore, the Ute women and children boarded a raft upon the lake. The storm grew worse, wind howling, waves rising, and even as the Ute warriors drove their enemies back over the divide, the women and children were swept to their deaths in the icy waters. It is said that if you step onto the lake during the winter and put your ear to the ice, you can still hear their cries.

Though questionable in their details, the legends reflect an underlying truth: The headwaters region of the Colorado was once a rich hunting ground, frequented and fought over by tribes from both sides of the mountains. A mining boom in the 1870s brought the first major influx of whites, but the boom went bust and Grand Lake became a tourist town. Developers built the Grand Ditch in the early 1890s, and diverted the headwaters on a larger scale half a century later to create a series of reservoirs on the river and its tributaries, pumping all but a minimal flow east of the mountains.

Ida Sheriff lives below those reservoirs near Hot Sulphur Springs, on a ranch her husband's family first homesteaded in 1881. A bright-eyed, white-haired woman with a quick sense of humor, Ida turns serious when she speaks of the river. "I remember when it really was a grand river," she says of the days before the dams. "Right now, you can wade across it." Ida explains that it's impossible to make a living as a rancher in Grand County, not only due to the water issues, but because of the short growing season and steep elevation. "In another 25 to 30 years, I don't think there'll be any ranches. We had to sell some of our land just to survive."

Not far from the Sheriff ranch, the Colorado flows through a small yet impressive canyon named after William N. Byers, a flamboyant Denver newspaper publisher who boosted development west of the mountains during the early days of statehood. It is the first of many canyons etched over eons into the western Rockies and the Colorado Plateau by a wilder, more powerful incarnation of the river. Across rugged rangelands and into redrock country, the Colorado winds through other canyons and wide open spaces until it reaches Moab, a green oasis in the Spanish Valley of southeastern Utah. Now the gateway to Arches and Canyonlands National Parks, the Moab area was sacred to two sophisticated and ancient Indian cultures, the Anasazi and the Fremont, who lived to the southeast and northwest respectively until a mysterious mass evacuation during the 13th century. These cultures met along the river, leaving rock art that still evokes a world of ritual magic and the awesome forces of the Earth.

Downstream from Moab, the Colorado has worked its own awesome forces on the land, creating a dense maze of deep, spectacular canyons that even today are among the most inaccessible regions of the United States. Non-Indian eyes first saw the Grand Canyon in 1540, when García López de Cárdenas, a captain in Coronado's search for the mythical Seven Cities of Cibola, gazed down from the rim; he reported that it was a "useless piece of country." Over two centuries later, in 1776, Spanish priest Francisco Garcés visited a Havasupai village near the bottom of the canyon and gave the name "Rio Colorado"—Red River—to the red-brown, sediment-rich waters.

Although a few others probed its boundaries, the Grand Canyon itself remained unexplored until 1869, when John Wesley Powell set off with nine other men in four boats down the Green River and into the Colorado. A self-taught naturalist who had lost the lower portion of his right arm at the Battle of Shiloh, Powell described wonders never seen before by whites, and some which may never be seen again. Glen Canyon—now drowned beneath a man-made lake ironically named in Powell's honor—entranced him as he floated downriver in early August. "Past these towering monuments, past these mounded billows of orange sandstone, past these oak-set glens, past these fern-decked alcoves, past these mural curves, we glide hour after hour, stopping now and then, as our attention is arrested by some new wonder...."

On August 13, their 82nd day on the rivers, the Powell expedition entered the Grand Canyon of the Colorado. "We are now ready to start on our way down to the Great Unknown....We are three-quarters of a mile in the depths of the earth, and the great river shrinks into insignificance, as it dashes its angry waves against the walls and cliffs, that rise to the world above; they are but puny ripples, and we but pigmies, running up and down the sands, or lost among the boulders."

INTO "THE GREAT UNKNOWN"

In 1869, one-armed John Wesley Powell floated the Colorado River through what he called "the Great Unknown"—the Grand Canyon's inner gorge. Here he confers with Tau-gu, a Paiute, during a second Colorado expedition in 1871-72.

In the days that followed, Powell and his men were pounded again and again by the "angry waves," tossed through treacherous rapids between sheer granite walls. Finally, on August 27, they reached a set of rapids that appeared so dangerous that three men decided to abandon the expedition and climb out of the canyon. Even Powell questioned the propriety of going on, but the depth of his dreams won out: "...for years I have been contemplating the trip. To leave the exploration unfinished, to say that there is a part of the canyon which I cannot explore ...is more than I am willing to acknowledge." In tragic irony, the men who abandoned the expedition were killed by Indians—while Powell and those who shot the rapids with him emerged safely from the canyon on August 29, ultimately acclaimed as heroes.

Powell saw no Indians within the Grand Canyon, though he found ruins of ancient settlements and even raided a garden along the north bank, stealing delicious green squash to supplement the expedition's soggy rations. Human habitation in the canyon dates back over 4,000 years, but today only the Havasupai—who played host to Padre Garcés in the 18th century—still live within Powell's "Great Unknown." Their home is the village of Supai in Havasu Canyon carved by Havasu Creek, whose color inspired the tribe's name, meaning "People of the Blue Green Waters."

There is no road to Supai, and though helicopter service is available, many prefer to walk the sublime and gradual seven-mile descent to the village, an island of green serenity watered by a sacred creek, surrounded by sacred walls of redrock and limestone. On a late Sunday afternoon, after a leisurely hike down the trail, I sit with Roland Manakaja, grandson of the last Havasupai chief and now the tribe's director of natural resources. In his official position, Manakaja deals with water rights, protection of sacred sites, and sightseeing flights over Havasupai land. Our talk, though, is of history—not the history found in books or uncovered by archaeologists, but the history told by the Havasupai and remembered on the rocky walls that surround their village.

"Up there," Manakaja says, pointing to a redrock wall, "is where the shaman Yahoya first came to sing his power songs. The Creator told him this valley already had power, and he didn't need the songs.... And there," he adds, pointing to two stone pillars on the curving edge of the same rock wall, "is where the two warriors who followed Yahoya still stand. When those rocks fall, the village will cease to exist." As the sunlight fades in the deep canyon, Manakaja points north, where Havasu

GLEN CANYON DAM—ARIZONA

Controlling the river upstream of the Grand Canyon, Glen Canyon Dam and its Lake Powell impact the Colorado so totally that one report stated simply: "The river is forever changed." Even now some environmentalists advocate breaching the dam.

Creek winds through Coyote Canyon toward the Colorado. "We call the Colorado River the Backbone, Hakatai. Our shamans used its waters for healing and ceremonies."

There are no shamans in Supai today, and Manakaja worries that his people are losing touch with the old ways. He suggests the flood that whipped down Havasu Creek in the spring of 1990 may have been a wake-up call from the Creator. "You can call it El Niño, but it's rain, whether they give it a name or not. It's God's way, and He's sometimes using that to chastise us, to try and warn us." If God must chastise the Havasupai, I wonder, what about the rest of us?

After the Grand Canyon, the Colorado flows toward the concrete monolith of Hoover Dam, where the rushing waters back up to form Lake Mead, largest man-made lake in the United States. Built during the Great Depression, the dam provides hydroelectric power for large areas of Nevada, Arizona, and southern California, while the lake, the river below it, and a network of canals snaking through the desert sends life-giving water to farms and cities throughout a vast, dry, inhospitable region.

Dreams of large-scale irrigation began during the California gold rush. By 1901, some 100,000 acres of California's once-barren Imperial Valley had been turned to productive farmland, thanks to the Colorado's magic touch. Yet magic brings risks, and four years later—before the Hoover Dam controlled its flow—the river broke through the headgates of the Imperial Valley Canal, flooding fields and homes before settling into a desert sink that became known as the Salton Sea. Once a recreational paradise, today it is a dying ecosystem of poisoned birds and rotting fish, a sea without outlet that was never supposed to be there in the first place. Some might say much the same about the sprawling cities of Los Angeles, San Diego, Las Vegas, and Phoenix: booming desert metropolises dependent on the Colorado River's overtaxed resources. Across the U.S.-Mexico border, farmers in Baja California also depend on the river and take what is left—in most years, an alkaline trickle that disappears into the earth 10 or 20 miles short of its goal in the Gulf of California.

That night, I linger on the dirt path outside Roland Manakaja's house. There are no street lights in Supai, and the twilight turns quickly to night. Winds begin to blow, dogs howl, a horse whinnies strangely in the distance. And then I see it: the Big Dipper emerging over Coyote Canyon, star by star, bigger and clearer than I have ever seen it before. It is tilted downward, toward the Colorado—the Backbone—hovering low in the sky as if waiting for the hand of the Creator to dip into the rushing waters and pour them over the land. To slake our thirst? To feed our farms and cities? To cleanse, baptize, or wash away? Only the Creator knows. ∎

TEXTURES OF TIME — GRAND CANYON, ARIZONA

Justly famed for its power and overwhelming scale, the Grand Canyon also is known for the simple elegance of lesser treasures, such as this Zen-like study of sunlight and elemental nature.

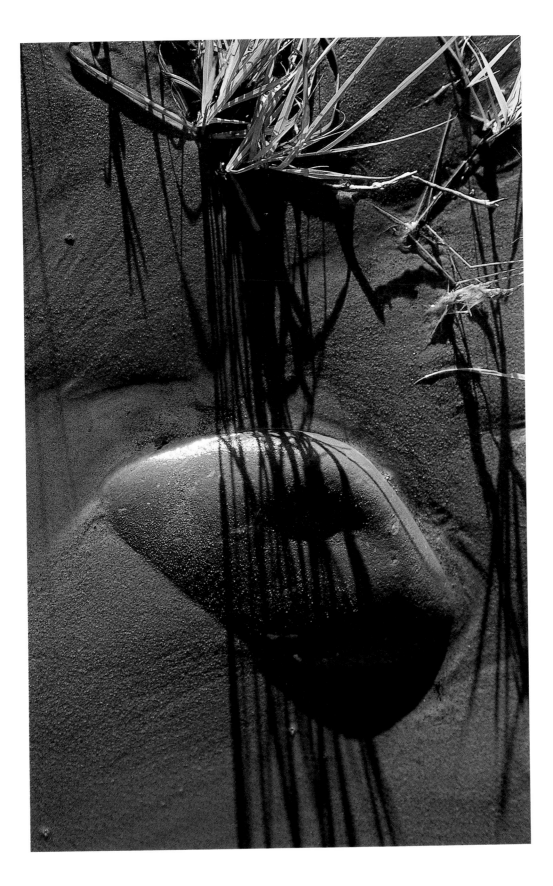

ROCKY MOUNTAIN NATIONAL PARK— COLORADO *Elk peacefully graze the bank*

upper Colorado River — once called the Grand — as it meanders through misty high country near its headwaters.

CANYONLANDS NATIONAL PARK—SOUTHERN UTAH

Merging waters as they carve their way through solid rock (below), the silt-laden Green River, at the left, and the equally erosive Colorado join forces in Canyonlands National Park.

LAKE POWELL—UTAH AND ARIZONA

Downstream from its confluence with the Green, the Colorado River begins to stall, its waters becoming flatter and bluer as sediments drop to the bottom and pleasure boaters proliferate (opposite). The slowdown is due to a 186-mile-long backup called Lake Powell, the result of Glen Canyon Dam, which began flooding the canyon in 1963, taming the wild river while promising huge recreational potential. Though meant to honor John Wesley Powell, it's doubtful that the rugged explorer would approve.

GRANITE GORGE — ARIZONA *Sentinel-like barrel cactuses stand guard amid the*

...ontories of Granite Gorge, a section of the Grand Canyon exposing rocks that date back two billion years.

CANYON COUNTRY—ARIZONA

Side canyons winding down to the Colorado offer a wealth of dreamlike worlds and magnificent landscapes, such as the mazy limestone narrows of Matkatamiba Canyon (opposite). River guide Martha Clark (below) kicks back in a travertine pool above Beaver Falls after a trying hike through another side canyon, carved by Havasu Creek.

FOLLOWING PAGES: COLORADO DELTA—MEXICO

Struggling to reach the sea, the Colorado—once a free-flowing carver of canyons— is now so used and abused by man that in all but the wettest years it disappears into alkaline flats 10 or 20 miles short of its natural destination: the Gulf of California.

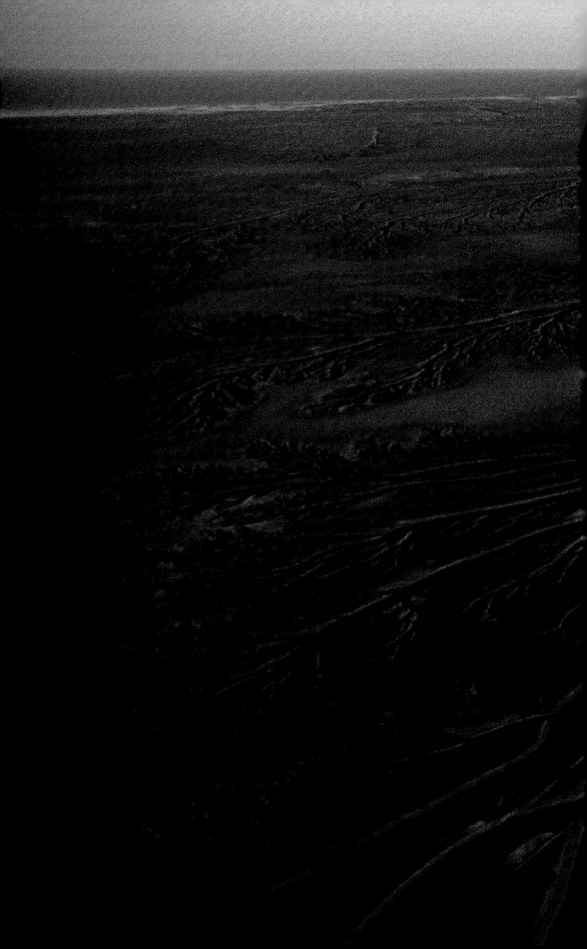

SACRAMENTO & SAN JOAQUIN

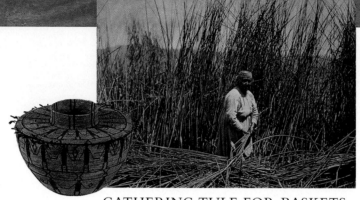

GATHERING TULE FOR BASKETS

■ HEADING EAST along a complex estuary their countrymen had named San Francisco, a Spanish expedition under Capt. Pedro Fages "ascended a pass to its highest point" and gazed eastward at a strange, bewildering network of rivers. It was near noon on March 30, 1772. Fages was looking for an inland route around San Francisco Bay, while Fray Juan Crespi, the Franciscan who accompanied him, was looking for souls. Crespi recorded the story:

"We saw that the land opened into a great plain as level as the palm of the hand.... Below the pass we beheld the estuary that we were following and saw that it was formed by two large rivers...that one of these rivers, the one to the south, was formed by two other rivers as wide as the principal one." Crespi believed that "these three arms of three large rivers were formed by a very large river, a league in width at least, which descended from some high mountains to the southeast, very far distant.... I gave to this great river the name of my Father San Francisco, so that he may intercede with His Divine Majesty for the conversion of all the immense body of heathen that no doubt must be on the banks of the great stream...."

Crespi's description is a bit confusing—after all, he was distracted by heathens—but the two large rivers must have been the Sacramento and the San Joaquin, while the third was probably the Mokelumne, all coming together in the great floodplain of the Sacramento-San Joaquin Delta. The stream he named "San Francisco"—today's San Joaquin—seemed the greatest of the trio due to his vantage point: the southeastern shore of Suison Bay, on a spur of Mount Diablo. The delta lay in the foreground before him, with the San Joaquin Valley and the Sierra Nevada beyond. In fact, the real powerhouse of this river system was and is the northern branch, all but unknown until 1808, when Spanish Lieutenant Gabriel Moraga explored it on horseback, and was so impressed by its pure, primeval beauty that he named it El Rio de los Sacramentos, after the Blessed Sacrament.

Nine years later, Don Luis Antonio Argüello, commandante of the San Francisco Presidio, pushed up the Sacramento in blunt-nosed boats rowed by coastal, Christianized Indians. He found a "king's park" lined with poplars, cottonwoods, alders, and oaks—many festooned with wild grapes. Lithe and quick-witted, Argüello was a second-generation Californian, born in the Presidio, and the Sacramento enchanted him, as did the grapes. He led another expedition three years later, marching up its western shore only to be turned back by hard going, low rations, and Indian arrows. Even on his deathbed, besotted by dreams and wine, Argüello spoke of the river as if it were the promised land, telling his confessor that he was going "up the smiling river to the north. It is a great river and I have a wish to see the beginning of it—I know it is born in the hills I saw that rise beyond."

And so it is, rising on the well-watered slopes of the Trinity Mountains in northern California and running east for a bit, picking up snowmelt from Mount Shasta before turning south for a long, straight run through the broad, fertile valley that bears its name—carrying a third of California's water on its way. The San Joaquin, born on the dry side of the Sierra, southeast of Yosemite National Park, has a more difficult route to the sea. It cuts a deep, spectacular canyon before finding a way through the mountains above present-day Fresno, where it turns toward the north, watering its own broad and fertile valley until it meets the Sacramento in the delta. Together, the Sacramento and San Joaquin Valleys form the great Central Valley of California, widely considered the most productive agricultural region in the world. And the richest soil of all is in the delta, low point of the valley, the heart of two great rivers.

Unlike the fan-shaped outward forming delta of the Mississippi, the delta of the Sacramento-San Joaquin formed inward, as sediments piled up behind the narrow Carquinez Straits. In these sediments grew rushes called tules, which decomposed to create organic peat soil up to 60 feet deep. When Europeans first saw it, the delta was a pristine wetland of a thousand square miles, with countless channels, tidal islands, and tule marshes—supporting a dizzying variety of wildlife. Otto von Kotzebue, who led a motley flotilla of Russian sailors and Aleutian kayakers here in 1824, reported "such a superfluity of game that those among us who had never been sportsmen before, when once they took a gun in hand, could not set it down for the sheer joy of it."

Two years after Kotzebue's expedition, American fur trappers led by Jedediah Smith crossed the desert into southern California and explored the Central Valley, testing tributaries of the San Joaquin and Sacramento not only for beaver but also for a way across the Sierra Nevada. Finally, on May 20, 1827, Smith and two companions headed up a tributary of the San Joaquin—apparently the Stanislaus—"and succeeded in crossing [the mountains] in eight days, having lost only two horses and one mule." It was the first crossing of the Sierra by white men, and it came from west to east.

After his return, Smith described "a country somewhat fertile, in which there were a great many Indians, mostly naked …[who] cut their hair to the length of three inches. They proved to be friendly. The manner of living is on fish, roots, acorns, and grass." These friendly, short-haired Indians were none other than "the immense body of heathen" that had caught Fray Crespi's imagination half a century before. In that time, they had lived on the edge of the Spanish mission world, occasionally supplying converts to work in the coastal missions, often harboring runaways who preferred their traditional lifestyle to Spanish doctrine. The runaways brought Spanish troops, but the real battle came in the summer of 1833, when a plague— probably malaria—swept down through the Central Valley, killing perhaps 20,000 of the 25,000 or so Indian people who lived there.

"From the extreme northern part of the Sacramento valley to the Tulare lake," wrote the companion of a trapper who passed through, "death had obtained a victory as unequalled, as it was unknown by nearly all, except the recording angel. Here and there,

SAN FRANCISCO BAY—AFTER THE 1849 GOLD RUSH

Deserted by gold-crazed crews gone to the hills, ships litter San Francisco Bay. Many vessels were dragged ashore and converted into makeshift warehouses, shops, and living space for the booming town.

near the mouth of the American river, and along the San Joaquin, the shadowy form, or ghostly figure could be seen, flitting through the forest, as if afraid of its own shadowless appearance. Not one female did we see. The numerous villages which we had left filled with life were converted into Golgothas.... The decaying bodies compelled us nightly to pitch our tents in the open prairie...."

Six years later, in August 1839, Swiss émigré John Augustus Sutter—with blessings from the Mexican governor and dreams of founding a utopian colony in the wilderness—sailed up the delta and into the unknown with two schooners and a rowboat, manned by an assortment of whites, Hawaiian servants, and an Indian boy. "I could find Nobody who could give me information," Sutter wrote, "only that they Knew that some very large rivers are in the interior…. It took me eight days before I could find the entrance of the Sacramento, as it is very deceiving and very easy to pass by." Once he found the river, Sutter worked his way to the confluence of the Sacramento and the American, a tributary named for Jedediah Smith's trappers. There he built a sprawling adobe fort, ultimately obtaining over 225 square miles of land from the Mexican government—a vast fiefdom he called New Helvetia.

"I had power of life and death over both Indians and white people," Sutter later boasted. But no power in the world could stop the mad stampede that began on January 24, 1848, when James Marshall found gold in the millrace of a sawmill he was building for Sutter on the South Fork of the American River, in an Edenic valley called

Coloma. At that time there were perhaps 14,000 non-Indians in California. By the end of 1849, there would be almost 100,000; three years later, a quarter million: all converging on "the Sacramento," a name that came to mean not just a river but a region, a land of golden dreams. "A frenzy seized my soul," wrote one early argonaut. "Piles of gold rose up before me at every step; castles of marble, dazzling the eye… thousands of slaves bowing to my beck and call; myriads of fair virgins contending with each other for my love… in short, I had a very violent attack of the gold fever."

Gold fever changed California forever—and spelled doom for most of the state's remaining Indians. As whites overran traditional tribal lands, Native Americans who didn't die from starvation or sickness were hunted down in "a war of extermination," according to one eyewitness, "shooting them down like wolves"—men, women, and children.

In 1769, when the Spanish first arrived, California had been home to perhaps 300,000 Indian people. By 1860 there were fewer than 30,000. Even that sad figure only begins to tell the story; according to the 1860 census, the southern delta that once supported Fray Crespi's "immense body of heathen," now held 40 Indians. A decade later there were only five.

Today, our boat pushes slowly up Lost Slough, between overgrown banks of willow and white alder that are hung with wild grapes and echo with songbirds.

"This is the old pristine delta," says Ed Littrell, a wildlife biologist for the California Department of Fish and Game, his hands on the wheel, watching carefully for snags in the shallow channel. Perched on the bow, I can imagine how Don Luis Argüello or John Sutter might have felt, pushing up a similar channel into the unknown. Lost Slough is a fortunate relic flowing between natural banks, tucked away in a far corner, relatively untouched by time.

The rest of the delta has not been so fortunate. Some 1,100 miles of man-made levees line its channels, a vast reworking of nature completed between 1850 and 1930. The islands formed by these levees hold rich peat soil, but farms here are sinking below water level, and the levees that protect them are in danger of collapse. The delta is also the heart of California's water supply, providing drinking water for some 22 million people, about two-thirds of the state's population.

These pressures have conspired to threaten the health of the complex delta ecosystem, home to 750 species of plants and animals, some two dozen of them threatened or endangered, some of them found nowhere else on Earth. Just a few years ago, the state of the delta was so desperate, and the conflicting interests of farmers, urban water suppliers, and environmentalists so volatile, that many observers considered the situation to be hopeless. Today, however, there is a new sense of possibility, born of an unprecedented partnership among the leading players in what is known as the CALFED Bay-Delta Program.

Initiated in 1995, CALFED aims to arrive at a consensual master plan that will include at least six key elements: water-use efficiency, levee-system integrity, ecosystem restoration, water transfers, watershed management, and water quality. Ed Littrell manages the wildlife aspect of a state program aimed at conserving and enhancing natural habitat along the banks of levees while also strengthening the levees themselves. It's one of many compromises envisioned under CALFED, and already some private agricultural districts are voluntarily enhancing the ecosystem on their levees.

Others, however, are not so cooperative. On one levee we see men burning new growth, the acrid smoke fouling the clear autumn air. Some districts, I'm told, want to keep levees bare so they don't have to deal with environmental laws. If there's no habitat, then there's no habitat to protect. In a 1996 interview, Lester Snow, executive director of CALFED, addressed the basic conflict in broader terms: "We are trying to build a process and build it in a glass house. I think at any given moment we could resort back to warfare."

It's a war we can't afford to fight, a battle we can't afford to lose. ■

SAN JOAQUIN VALLEY — FRESNO, CALIFORNIA
One of the "California Raisins" makes a promotional appearance at the Raisin Bowl in Fresno, the self-proclaimed Raisin Capital of the World, which produces over 90 percent of America's raisins.

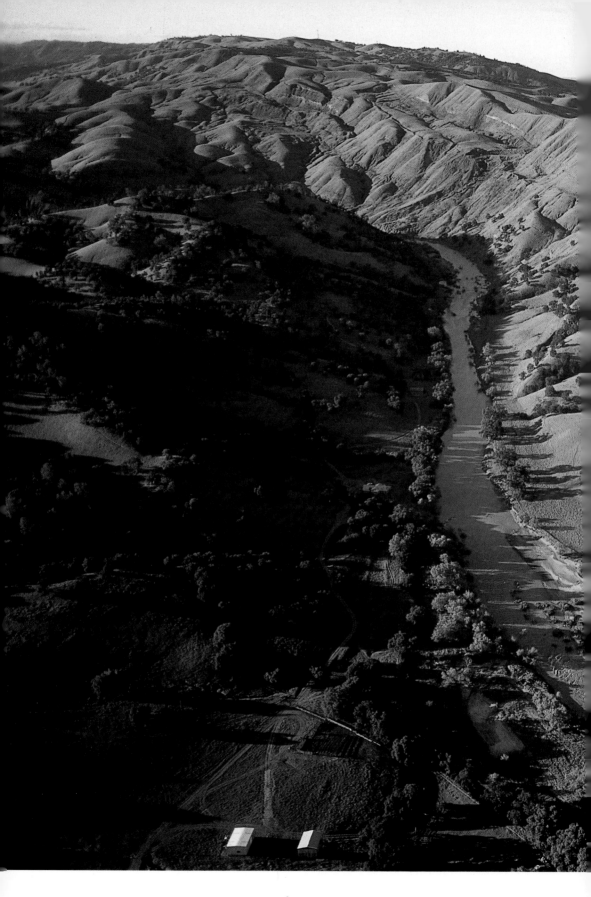

SACRAMENTO VALLEY—NORTHERN CALIFORNIA *Green hills flank an upper port*

Sacramento—River of the Sacraments—which carries almost a third of the state's runoff to the sea.

SAN LUIS N.W.R. — SAN JOAQUIN RIVER, CALIFORNIA

Avocets gather in restored wetlands of the Kesterson Unit of the San Luis National Wildlife Refuge (opposite), located along the San Joaquin west of Merced. Some 95 percent of the Central Valley's wetlands have been drained for agriculture, putting pressures on these and other migratory bird populations.

CITY OF SACRAMENTO, CALIFORNIA

State capital and historic gateway to the goldfields, Sacramento rose from a riverbank town to become a modern metropolis with a palpable sense of the past (below). Today, against a backdrop of skyscrapers, excursion boats ply the river that gave the city its name.

FIELDS OF PLENTY—NEAR FIREBAUGH, CALIFORNIA

Once largely barren desert, Fresno County now produces more than
250 agricultural products—more than any other county in America. This bounty is
only possible with the water of the San Joaquin River. Cantaloupe harvesters (below)
work a farm near Firebaugh that also raises tomatoes and cotton,
while another farm worker (opposite) sprays strawberries protected by plastic sheeting.

FOLLOWING PAGES: ORCHARD—FRESNO COUNTY

Like a grid of snowflakes, blooming fruit trees pattern an orchard in Fresno County, known for its abundant groves. Named for the Spanish word for ash tree, the county was organized in 1856 on the heels of California's gold rush; the city of Fresno took shape in 1872, thanks to the arrival of the Central Pacific Railroad.

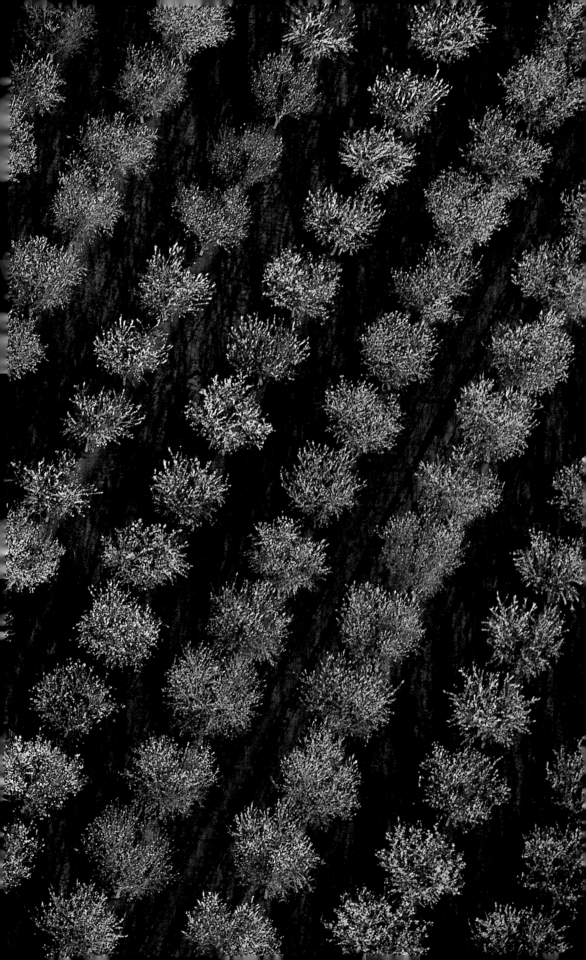

COLUMBIA

APPLE COUNTRY—WASHINGTON STATE

■ THE MOUTH OF THE COLUMBIA churns below me, but I can barely see it, just a curving sliver of whitecaps crashing on a rocky beach 80 feet beneath the cliff on which I stand. Wind and rain beat hard against my face, and as I gaze toward the Pacific—invisible in gray-blue rain and fog—I imagine the Columbia Bar laying in wait for careless sailors. Created by the West's most powerful river, deposited in a mouth so wide it was once mistaken for the ocean, the Columbia Bar and surrounding headlands have wrecked some 2,000 ships in two centuries of exploration and commerce. Even today, the area's ruthless winds and currents make this the most dangerous river mouth in the United States, third most dangerous in the world, and it is a point of pride among professional sailors to be a Columbia River Bar pilot.

There were no experienced pilots to be had in the late 18th century, when Spanish and British ships first probed the rain-soaked, rocky North Pacific coast in their search for a mythical water route called variously the Northwest Passage, the Strait of Anian, or the River of the West. "These currents and the seething of the waters have led me to believe that it may be the mouth of some great river or some passage to another sea," wrote Spanish captain Bruno de Heceta, anchored off the bar in August 1775. Yet the map he drew shows not a river but a bay, for with his crew suffering from scurvy and his eye deeming the currents too treacherous to pass, Heceta sailed on toward the south. In 1788, British trader John Meares grew so frustrated by the steady surf breaking over the bar that he decided, "no such river…exists, as laid down in the Spanish charts." He named the "bay" Deception and called its rocky headland Cape Disappointment.

British naval captain George Vancouver noted "the appearance of an inlet, or small river" in the spring of 1792 but continued onward, "not considering this opening worthy of more attention." Just two weeks later, on May 12, 1792, American merchant captain Robert Gray—more interested in furs than mythical passages— "saw an apearance of a spacious harbour abrest the ship," according to one of his crew, "haul'd our wind for it, observ'd two sand bars making off, with a passage between them to a fine river…. We directed our course up this noble river in search of a Village." Gray crossed the bar and spent eight days trading for sea otter and beaver pelts amid the towering rain forest, while his men enjoyed the sexual favors of "very pretty" Indian women. He named the river after his ship, *Columbia Rediviva*, and sailed back over the bar, ultimately heading for China to trade his pelts for tea.

That fall Vancouver returned, armed with a chart drawn by Gray. Still unable to enter the Columbia in his own large ship, he sent an accompanying brig across the bar under Lt. William Broughton—who sailed a hundred miles upriver, where he invited an old Indian chief on board and "formally took possession of the river, and the country in its vicinity, in his Britannic Majesty's name, having every reason to believe, that the subjects of no other civilized nation or state had ever entered into this river before." Broughton conveniently ignored Gray's efforts, while the old Indian and the people he represented were hardly civilized in the eyes of an 18th-century Englishman. He had no way of knowing that the Columbia had been home to human culture for 11,000 years. Nor did he know that beyond the magnificent gorge that impeded his progress was a set of wild rapids, Celilo Falls, with a nearby fishing village where human beings had lived and loved and honored their Creator for the past 8,000 years—the oldest continuously inhabited community in North America.

Lewis and Clark reached Celilo Falls from the east on October 22, 1805, the second year of their epic journey to the Pacific. "At the lower part of those rapids," wrote Clark, "we arrived at 5 Large Lod[g]es of nativs drying and prepareing fish for market, they gave us Philburts, and berries to eate." The Indians aided the explorers in portaging around the falls, carrying heavy articles on their horses, even catching one of the canoes when the elkskin rope that held it broke. But they were unwilling to part with their precious salmon, for this was the time of storing food for the winter. Instead, they sold the travelers "8 Small fat dogs…the flesh of which the most of the party have become fond of from the habits of useing it for Some time past."

The expedition continued to an even wilder rapids, where Clark "deturmined to pass through…notwithstanding the horrid appearance of this agitated gut swelling, boiling & whorling in every direction." And so they did, safely shooting the treacherous waters to the astonishment of the Indians watching from the rock above. Next day, they shot another set of rapids, and on November 1, the Americans portaged yet another to the west, where the river opens into the broad, foggy, tidal channel that Lieutenant Broughton had claimed for Britain 13 years before.

Although their journals don't reflect its majesty, Lewis and Clark were the first whites to traverse the Columbia Gorge, cut by the great river through the volcanic Cascade Mountains. Young by geological standards, the gorge has the painfully beautiful sheen of a land just touched by Creation, a place of startling transition in climate, landscape, and culture. "It looks like God just stopped and took a rest," says one longtime resident—and so it does, if your God is a God of rain and rocks. On the

141

western side, where the Bonneville Dam now straddles the river, craggy cliffs are crowded with tall hemlock and Douglas fir, dissected by spectacular falls, fed by 75 inches of rain each year. Just 45 miles to the east, the bald and rounded sagebrush hills above the Dalles—not far from old Celilo Falls—receive only 14 inches.

The gorge connected two great Indian cultures: the wealthy trading peoples of the Pacific Northwest and the poorer yet powerful tribes of the Columbia Plateau. Traveling in big wooden canoes, living in wooden houses, wearing hats of bark to protect them from the rain, the coastal Indians valued wealth and commerce—as did the Americans and the British traders who supplanted them. By the time Lewis and Clark arrived, over a hundred American ships had followed Robert Gray across the bar, spreading manufactured goods that soon changed the coastal culture, and diseases that had already killed between one-third and one-half of the precontact population. Yet they kept trading—salmon, furs, even their daughters. By 1841, the death toll among local tribes approached 92 percent.

Indians east of the gorge were more careful in trade, more focused on their own survival and on the great river, Nch'i-Wana, that brought them life in a vast, semi-arid land. They lived in mat lodges, traveled in smaller canoes, and rode horses over the broken hills beyond its shores. Heading home in April 1806, Lewis and Clark visited Celilo Falls again, and reported "great joy with the natives last night in consequence of the arrival of the Salmon; one of those fish was caught; this was the harbinger of good news to them…this fish was dressed and being divided into small peices was given to each child in the village." This was the First Fish Ceremony, central sacrament of the old Washani religion of the Columbia Plateau.

During the decades that followed, white influence gradually permeated the plateau, first from trappers, then from missionaries, finally from settlers and soldiers. In 1847, a wagon train on the Oregon Trail brought measles to the Whitman Mission, on the Yakima River near its confluence with the Columbia. Marcus Whitman, a doctor as well as a missionary, treated sick emigrants and the local Cayuse Indians who became infected, despite his knowledge of a deeply held Cayuse belief that a shaman who loses his patient must pay with his life. And so Whitman paid—with a tomahawk through his skull—after half the tribe died of the mysterious disease. His wife and 12 other whites died with him. The following year the sprawling Oregon Territory, first official territory west of the Rockies, was formed—in part to capture the murderers. One of them, Cayuse chief Tiloukaikt, said as he faced the noose in 1850: "Did not your missionaries tell us that Christ died to save his people? So die we, to save our people."

By that time there were 12,000 whites in the territory, most in the fertile Willamette Valley west of the Cascades. Of the approximately 50,000 Indians who had inhabited the Columbia basin when Gray first crossed the bar, perhaps a thousand remained on the lower river, with a few thousand more along the upper river beyond the gorge. Their last stand began in 1855, after Isaac Stevens, governor of the newly formed Washington Territory, negotiated a treaty with plateau tribes and broke his word

12 days later. Fighting raged across the rugged land until artillery and long-range rifles blasted the tribes off the Spokane Plain in September 1858.

In the midst of this chaos and transition, a powerful voice emerged as if from the river itself: the voice of Smohalla, a dreamer-prophet who lived at a place whites called Priest Rapids on a desolate stretch of the Columbia some 400 miles from the sea. Smohalla's people, the Wanapum—River People—fought no wars, signed no treaties, and refused to move onto reservations. Protected by their isolation, inspired by dreams and songs and sacred dance, they revitalized the Washani religion of harmony with Mother Earth. "We simply take the gifts that are freely offered," Smohalla told an Army officer in the late 1880s. "We no more harm the earth than would an infant's fingers harm its mother's breast. But the white man tears up large tracts of land, runs deep ditches, cuts down forests, and changes the whole face of the earth. You know very well this is not right."

SALMON FISHING ALONG THE COLUMBIA

Poised just downstream from Kettle Falls in northeastern Washington, Colville Indians use three traditional methods—the club, the gig, and the trap—to catch spawning salmon in this paint-ing by Paul Kane, an Irish-born Canadian artist who traveled the Columbia in 1846-47. Jesuit missionary Pierre DeSmet wrote, "It was a common occurrence...to take three thousand salmon in a day" at the falls, one of over a hundred rapids and waterfalls that, in his words, made the Columbia "undoubtedly the most dangerous river on the western side of the American hemisphere." Today, all the Columbia's rapids have been silenced by dams— and the annual salmon run is but a shadow of what it once was.

Today, just a century later, we have changed the face of the Earth in ways that even Smohalla saw only in dreams, if at all. Fourteen massive dams have turned the once-mighty Nch'i-Wana into a series of placid lakes; the once-raging cataracts of the Columbia Gorge have been silenced, the ancient village of Celilo Falls drowned beneath dammed waters. And though we depend on energy supplied by the dams and eat fruits of the fields they irrigate, we have begun to see—as Smohalla saw—that it is not right. We spend about 300 million dollars each year trying to save the waning salmon, and recently there is talk of breaching dams, if not on the Columbia at least on some of its tributaries, to help the salmon reestablish themselves. There are even those who suggest that this river has a right to be a river—wild, free, unconstrained.

Smohalla's village is gone now, but the Wanapum still live at Priest Rapids in a dozen neat wooden houses tucked behind Priest Rapids Dam. Their leader is Rex Buck, great grandnephew of Smohalla, a round-faced man with a ready smile and long black braids, guiding the Wanapum in the ways of the Washani religion. Rex works at the dam, supervising electrical maintenance of the huge turbines. Though aware of the irony, he sees his role at the dam and the role of the Wanapum in strangely parallel terms.

"Just like this dam needs maintenance in order to continue producing," he says, voice carrying over the turbines, "the Wanapum need maintenance within themselves so they can continue to make that beautiful sound that this river makes.... We can't go back to the way we were. There's no room. It's not there. But we can maintain it with what little bit is left.... We're not here so we can become rich, or because the federal government owes us something, or the utility district owes us something. We're here to take care of what our parents, grandparents, and ancestors took care of, that we can pass that on to our children, that our children will pass that on to their children...that those things will always be maintained as the Creator gave them to us."

That evening I watch the sunset from desert hills 18 miles up the Columbia, where yet another dam—named after the Wanapum—now zigzags from shore to shore, the water above it turning from shimmering silver to midnight blue as pink clouds reflect in its glassy surface.

I wonder what it was like to watch this river in its glory, when 16 million salmon thronged its channel, when Lewis and Clark ran its rapids, when Smohalla preached along its shores. Then I think of Rex Buck and the Wanapum who still find a way to live in this place—not as it was but as it is—and it strikes me that the true power of a river cannot be measured by the strength of its flow or the size of its salmon run. The power lies deeper, in the soul of the river itself and the spirit of the people who love it. ■

PETROGLYPH—COLUMBIA GORGE, WASHINGTON

Known as She Who Watches, this petroglyph gazes over what was called the Long Narrows or Great Dalles of the Columbia, once a thriving trading center for Indians from both the upper and lower river.

GRAND COULEE DAM—WASHINGTON *Water cascades over the man-made spillway at G*

...ulee, which helps irrigate an area as big as Rhode Island and can generate enough electricity for six Seattle-size cities.

HARVESTING THE COLUMBIA — *Gaffing a prized king salmon, this Yakima Indian follows*

-old tradition reaffirmed by an 1855 treaty that guaranteed natives the right to fish at all "usual and accustomed" places.

MULTNOMAH FALLS — COLUMBIA GORGE

With a dramatic double drop totaling 620 vertical feet, Multnomah Falls ranks among the highest waterfalls in the United States. Benson Bridge, built by Italian stonemasons in 1914, stands between the upper and lower cataracts. In 1995, a 400-ton boulder plunged from the upper rock face into a pool below, splashing water and debris up and over the bridge. That rockfall and a more recent landslide are part of the natural erosion process that created Multnomah Falls in the first place.

CATCHING THE WIND — COLUMBIA GORGE

*Gouged out by the once-wild river, Columbia Gorge provides windsurfers with a
natural wind tunnel through the Cascades. The town of Hood River, Oregon, located in the heart of
the gorge, has become a major outfitting center for the sport, while an annual event
known as the Gorge Games focuses on varied outdoor competitions that include not only
windsurfing but also parasailing, sky surfing, kayaking, mountain biking, and
snowboarding, drawing enthusiasts from around the globe.*

PORTLAND, OREGON

Commercial center of the lower Columbia, Oregon's queen city of Portland (below) thrives where the Willamette River meets the Columbia. The latter river links Portland and other inland cities to the Pacific Ocean, providing passage for all sorts of commerce, including the massive rafts of logs (opposite) that attest to the nation's largest lumber industry.

FOLLOWING PAGES:
ASTORIA, OREGON

Ghostly pilings rise from the shallows beneath Astoria Bridge, recalling days when the town of Astoria—near the mouth of the mighty Columbia—was a booming salmon canning center. Today, the canneries are gone, but tourists visit the quaint Victorian town for its historic museums and nearby Fort Clatsop, where Lewis and Clark spent a long, wet winter at the end of their journey to the Pacific.

■ NOTHING VISIBLE in the surrounding terrain suggests a river should be here. No stupendous mountains or rocky ramparts or glacial valleys melting of ice and snow. Yet here it is, an allegory of patience and persistence, a symbol of the subarctic; nearly a mile wide and bound for the sea, moving with quiet determination at three or four knots. Not easy to paddle a canoe against. But what a ride to go with it, to travel unfettered on the back of the beast, like Alexander Mackenzie in 1789, or Klondike gold dreamers in 1898, or native hunters and fisherfolk centuries before. Everything about this river implies vastness and distance and the inertia of a hundred upstream tributaries, the anguish and joys of lives now gone. All that water and not a sound. Not a riffle or a rapid. Just silence, a silence so deep and timeless it stretches as far away as my imagination — farther.

A raptor flies by, a northern harrier, formerly called a marsh hawk. It too, as if in consonance with the river, is silent. It moves close to the ground over moose tracks in the near-shore mud, passing grasses rich with rodents, its favorite prey. Beyond the shore a forest of spruce and birch trees flanks steep bluffs and escarpments. And beyond that, mystery; millions of acres of mystery. This northern river country — the watershed of both the Yukon and the Mackenzie, each an icon of wildness — has been thoroughly mapped. And the maps have a lot to say. But they don't tell the dramas of wildlife migrations and lightning fires, of summer's burning heat and winter's bitter cold, of lives saved and lost, of the legends of the Dene, Inuit, Gwich'in, Koyukon, Yup'ik, and others who have lived here for more generations than can be

■ *KIM HEACOX* ■

counted. For them, the elders at least, the oldest maps are not maps at all, but are dreams of hunting, trapping, berry picking, and caring for each other; of sleeping on the ground and waking to the frosty stillness of a heaven on Earth.

The spine of the Rocky Mountains separates the Yukon from the Mackenzie—Yukon to the west, Mackenzie to the east—yet they are sibling rivers. Each is long and large and undefiled by even a single dam. Each is an important home and highway for those northerners who inhabit its shores. Born from glacial meltwaters above Atlin Lake, in British Columbia, the Yukon travels some 2,000 miles through the Yukon Territory and across Alaska. At Fort Yukon it kisses the Arctic Circle, then turns west-southwest to eventually spill into the Bering Sea. The Mackenzie begins at Great Slave Lake, in Canada's Northwest Territories, flows west, then turns north at Camsell Bend and continues to the Beaufort Sea, part of the Arctic Ocean. Alexander Mackenzie called it the "River Disappointment," as he had hoped it would take him west to the Pacific Ocean and provide an important fur-trading route. Most Klondike stampeders might have called the Yukon the same thing—disappointing—for when they arrived in the boomtown of Dawson City they learned that all the good mining claims had been staked.

These men brought with them great expectations, but the north country saw no reason to oblige them. For those who stayed, however, the rivers would offer a deeper wealth, something as simple as fresh fish and friendly neighbors. It turned out that the best riches, like the best gifts, weren't taken. They were received. And the best of all, given.

OGILVIE MOUNTAINS — YUKON TERRITORY *Amber sunset warms the granite spires of Mo*

...molith in the Tombstone Range of the Ogilvie Mountains, which divide the drainages of the Yukon and Mackenzie Rivers.

YUKON

KLONDIKE PERFORMERS — DAWSON, YUKON TERRITORY

■ OLD TIMERS SAY summer is a beautiful lie, that winter is the truth about the Yukon. Everything in summer lives in response to winter, they say, and they should know. They have lived along this ancient, defiant river for ten thousand perfect days and ten thousand perfect nights — and more.

Ducks on the wing, grayling on the rise, salmon in the nets, berries on the bush: so many fleeting gifts to be celebrated. No sooner does summer get its momentum up then wham, it shuts down. The air turns chilly in August. Birch leaves blanket the ground in September. A first snow paints the hilltops with a white patina that appears like powdered sugar, what locals call "termination dust."

Come November, the air temperature might fall to 40 degrees below zero. But a river this size — nearly a mile across — takes a while to freeze. Bitter cold to the touch but not yet frozen, the water is 70 degrees warmer than the air. Steam rises off it as if it were boiling. Amber morning light spills through the naked trees. Smoke spirals up from a log cabin in the woods on shore. Inside, sourdough pancakes cook over a wood-burning stove. Another winter is about to begin along the most famous river in northwestern North America, a river nearly 2,000 miles long (1,400 of those miles in Alaska). The garden is in, the root cellar full. Firewood has been bucked up and split. A bull moose has been shot; the meat cured. Hundreds of frozen chum salmon have been stacked like cordwood to feed the huskies through winter. The propane tank is full. Novels and books of essays crowd the shelves. Winter? Bring it on. Let it snow and blow.

For many of the 36,000 people who live along this river (two-thirds of them in Whitehorse, capital city of Canada's Yukon Territory), wealth is not strictly a matter of money but of how you conduct yourself; of having skills and friends and a sense of place. Downstream, in Alaska, 24 villages nestle along this river, only two with road access to the outside world. The others are reached year-round by boat or plane, or now and then by the intrepid traveler on foot, skis, or dogsled.

Any river so long cannot escape a profound history; in this case a history spoken long before it was written, passed down from mother to daughter for countless generations. Story anchored people to their past and gave reverence to their way of life. In the upper Yukon, these people were the Nacho Nyak Dun; in interior Alaska they were the Koyukon and Tananahan Athapaskans; near the Bering Sea along the lower Yukon River, they were the Yup'ik Eskimos. Their distant ancestors had crossed the Bering Land Bridge when glacial ice dominated much of North America and the sea level was lower, enabling people to walk from Siberia to Alaska. These first North Americans lived by hunting, fishing, and gathering berries and other foods. To this day, subsistence remains a viable and valuable way of life here, and people follow the seasons closely.

In the Yup'ik language, April is *Maklagaq*, meaning baby bearded seals. May is *Irniviat Tengmiat*, meaning the birds have their young. August is *Nurarcurvik*—time to hunt caribou calves; December is *Cauyarvik*—the month for playing drums. And January, the coldest and bleakest month of all, is *Iralull'eq*—the bad month.

Anthropologist and author Richard Nelson, who lived among the Koyukon people of interior Alaska, wrote, "Known places on the landscape have a multitude of associations with hunting events or animal experiences. When Koyukon people traverse the country, their recollection of these events not only gives the land meaning but also perpetuates useful knowledge for locating resources and finding the way from place to place."

Contact with white men first occurred around 1790, when Russian traders traveled overland from Iliamna Lake, across the Kuskokwim River and into the Yukon drainage. Nearly half a century later, the Russian-American Company built fur-trading posts north and south of the mouth of the Yukon. Kenneth L. Pratt, an anthropologist with the Bureau of Indian Affairs, has written: "In addition to encouraging exploration of the region, the development of Russian-American Co. trading posts ultimately resulted in a reorientation of the Eskimos' primary trade channels and resource harvesting strategies...and led to intermarriage between Russian men and local women." Still, there were cultural chasms, polarized values, and—most damaging of all—diseases. Despite Russian attempts to vaccinate the Eskimos, a smallpox epidemic swept the region in 1838-39. Kuskokwim Eskimos retaliated by destroying the trading post at Ikogmiut.

In 1845 the Russian Orthodox Church arrived in the form of priests who calmly supervised the reconstruction of Ikogmiut, today's Russian Mission. They lived among the Eskimos and incorporated them into church organization. To this day, Russian Orthodoxy has a strong presence in the area, despite the fact that Russia sold Alaska to the United States back in 1867 (for 7.2 million dollars, roughly two cents an acre).

Like most North American rivers, the history of the Yukon was painted in gradual brush strokes of discovery, conflict, and integration. But here those strokes were eclipsed by the grand flourish of the Klondike gold rush, one of the largest human movements of modern times. "GOLD! GOLD! GOLD! GOLD!" read the headline on a special edition of the Seattle *Post-Intelligencer* on July 17, 1897. "68 Rich

Men on the Steamer *Portland* STACKS OF YELLOW METAL." One clever reporter coined the phrase, "a ton of solid gold," and it sailed around the nation, electrifying down-on-their-luck dreamers from California to Connecticut.

The winter of 1897-98 saw tides of hungry men—and a few women—forsake their pasts to journey north and reinvent themselves in the bitter snows of the Chilkoot and White Passes, hauling supplies from coastal Alaska into Canada's Yukon Territory. On the shores of inland mountain lakes they felled trees to build makeshift boats, then waited for the ice to go out, so they could travel down the Yukon River to Dawson City, heart of the Klondike. In late May 1898, it happened.

"Within forty-eight hours all the lakes were clear of ice," wrote Pierre Berton in *The Klondike Fever,* "and the whole freakish flotilla of 7,124 boats loaded with thirty million

ROBERT SERVICE REMEMBERED — DAWSON

Born in England, reared in Scotland, and eventually a resident of France,
Robert Service will be forever remembered as the bard of the Yukon. Traveling through Canada's Yukon
Territory as a young man in the early 1900s, he wrote numerous poems that encapsulated the
lifestyle and sense of humor that ruled the area during its gold-rush days.
Among his most memorable: The Cremation of Sam McGee, The Shooting of Dan McGrew,
and The Spell of the Yukon, *here excerpted on the side of a historic building*
in Dawson, overlooking the Yukon River.

pounds of solid food was in motion.... Off they sailed like miniature galleons, seeking the treasure that lay beyond the horizon's rim, the most bizarre fleet ever to navigate fresh water. Here were twenty-ton scows crammed with oxen, horses, and dogs, one-man rafts made of three logs hastily bound together, light Peterborough canoes packed over the passes on men's shoulders, and strange oblong vessels that looked like—and sometimes were—floating packing-boxes.... Here were skiffs and cockleshells, outriggers and junks, catamarans and kayaks, arks and skiffs, catboats and wherries. Here were boats with wedge bottoms, and boats with flat bottoms, and boats with curved bottoms; boats shaped like triangles and boats shaped like circles; boats that looked like coffins and boats that were coffins. Here were enormous rafts with hay and horses aboard, propelled by mighty sweeps; and here were others built from a single log with only a mackinaw coat for a sail.... And here was a boat with two women who had sewed their undergarments together and suspended them between a pair of oars to make a sail."

First came Miles Canyon, then Squaw Rapids and White Horse Rapids, "so called," wrote Berton, "because the foam upon them resembled white steeds leaping and dancing in the sunlight." The river narrowed to one-third its width as it funneled through the basalt gauntlet. The first boats, refusing to surrender their positions, ran the rapids and paid the price: 150 boats wrecked, 10 men drowned. Thereafter, a Mountie named Sam Steele arrived and issued an order: Women and children would walk the five miles around the rapids, and every boat would be piloted by a helmsman who knew what he was doing. Anyone who disobeyed would pay a fine of one hundred dollars. The accidents ended. And an enterprising young man built a tram around the rapids, proving as had others before him that those who often made the most money from a gold rush were the ones who mined the miners.

Most men found little or no gold, yet in their later years said the gold rush was the most exciting time in their lives. In his signature poem, *The Spell of the Yukon*, Robert Service wrote:

There's gold, and it's haunting
and haunting;
It's luring me on as of old;
Yet it isn't the gold that I'm wanting
So much as just finding the gold.
It's the great, big,
broad land 'way up yonder,
It's the forests where silence has lease;
It's the beauty that thrills me
with wonder,
It's the stillness
that fills me with peace.

The first town on the river after it departs Canada for Alaska is Eagle, made famous in John McPhee's 1976 book, *Coming into the Country*. "With a clannish sense of place characteristic of the bush," wrote McPhee, "people in the region of the upper Yukon refer to their part of Alaska as 'the country.' A stranger appearing among them is said to have 'come into the country.'" Then—as now—people prided themselves on a fierce independence and self-reliance. They built their own cabins, planted and harvested their own gardens, and schooled their kids at the kitchen table. McPhee described one tough homesteader, Dick Cook, as being "below the threshold of slender. He is fatless. His figure is a little stooped, unprepossessing, but his legs and arms are strong beyond the mere requirements of the athlete. He looks like a scarecrow made of cables." Cook did it all: hunted, trapped, fished, mined. "With no trouble at all, Dick Cook remembers where every trap is on his lines. He uses several hundred traps. His annual food cost is somewhere under a thousand dollars. He uses less than a hundred gallons of fuel—for his chain saws, his small outboards, his gasoline lamps. The furs bring him a little more than his basic needs—about fifteen hundred dollars a year. He plants a big garden. He says, 'One of the points I live by is not to make any more money than is absolutely necessary.'"

I first met the Yukon River in winter, during the Iditarod Trail Sled Dog Race, which runs from Anchorage northwest to Nome, some 1,100 miles over ice and snow. Approaching a village at midnight, each musher appeared as nothing more than a single headlamp moving through an immense darkness. The sky was clear and bright with a million stars, and northern lights flickered through the Big Dipper. Villagers waited at the town entrance bundled in their parkas, children atop their fathers' shoulders, eyes wide with anticipation, their vaporous breaths rising in the frigid air. When a musher finally arrived, his moustache and eyelashes caked with ice, everybody gathered around to admire and listen, to pat him on the back and confirm the bonds that make the Yukon River home. I thought then as I do now, that in such big country it's the cold that makes people warm, the distances that make them close. People think little of jumping on a snowmobile and traveling at breakneck speeds for a hundred miles, simply to see a friend. In summer they do it by motorboat, often just as fast.

Many modern conveniences have come to the Yukon—microwaves, chainsaws, televisions, satellite dishes, medical clinics, high-performance engines—some more eagerly embraced than others. Things aren't as quiet as they used to be, or as slow. As one man said to me in Ruby years ago, "Everybody in the city has them modern time-saving devices, and some folks got 'em out here. But do they have more time? I don't think so."

It doesn't take much for native villagers to slip from one world back into another. When somebody announced over a CB radio that a bearded seal was in the river near the Yup'ik village of Alakanuk, every able-bodied man and boy jumped to his feet—some abandoning television shows—grabbed a darting harpoon or a throwing board, and joined the hunt. Working together in boats, they pursued and killed the seal, and hauled it to shore. There, beaming with tribal pride, they divided up the meat and fat under the supervision of elders. It was times like this, not in front of a television, when the ethnic meaning of Yup'ik—"real person"—had its greatest depth.

I remember a village woman who was so grateful to see her husband and son return home safely and successfully from a hunt that she cried tears of joy. Not only had the two men in her life returned to her, they had enough moose meat in tow to get the family through the long winter. Possible meals on the menu that year included moose steak, moose roast, moose stew, moose meatloaf, Swiss moosesteak, moose-burgers, fried moose liver, ground moose in Spanish rice, moose sandwiches and soup, and—not to be forgotten—leftover moose.

She later told me that a large bull moose can weigh over 1,000 pounds; the four dressed quarters, 700 pounds. Deduct for trim and bones and you get around 400 pounds of meat, enough to sustain a family of six through the winter. For hobby hunters from Fairbanks or Anchorage who fly into the country to get their moose, then return home to high-paying government or private-sector jobs, the meat is

CHILKOOT PASS, ALASKA — 1898 GOLD RUSH

Thousands of would-be millionaires climbed the rocky funnel they called "the Scales"
in the Chilkoot Pass, gateway to the Yukon. Canadian Mounties at the pass enforced a strict law:
Every man and woman entering Canada had to bring at least a ton of supplies,
a rule that required each of them to make as many as 40 trips up
and down the Scales. To prevent theft, gold stampeders often worked in teams,
one climbing while the other guarded the supplies.

pure gravy. But for subsistence families living by their wits and skills in the bush along the Yukon, a moose is as essential as good bread and water.

Spring on the upper Yukon comes in April and May, a time called breakup, when great slabs of ice groan and rumble, and at times explode apart with sounds like cannon fire. The ice moves downstream, breaking free as the river again becomes fluid. Bets abound on what day, hour, and minute breakup will occur. The most famous bet, the Nenana Ice Classic, involves a large tripod set on the Tanana River, a tributary of the Yukon. A tripwire runs from the tripod to the town of Nenana. The minute the tripod moves, signaling breakup, the clock stops. Since 1918, the winning times have been between April 20 and May 20. Winners divide a large purse. Yet each year a few absent-minded people have no chance of winning. They bet on April 31, a date that doesn't exist.

I once followed the Yukon in a small plane in May, flying from the interior settlement of Tanana hundreds of miles downriver to the mouth. It was only two days, but it appeared as if I had traveled back in time two months. In Tanana, the river was free of ice. The buds were open. Not far away, clouds of birds were arriving at the 8.6-million acre Yukon Flats National Wildlife Refuge, one of the richest waterfowl areas in the United States, home to millions of nesting ducks and geese. But as I flew downriver, the land turned from green to brown, then white. Floating ice filled the river from bank to bank and rafted into a massive jam near the mouth, still frozen solid. And the Bering Sea also, as far as I could see, was white with snow and ice.

Winter is never far away here. Neither is the past. Michael Parfit wrote in NATIONAL GEOGRAPHIC magazine about canoeing past "a ghostly superstructure rising out of woods on an island. This whole section of the river was as eerie as an overgrown Inca temple…. As a recent traveler wrote, the place was like a stage on which 'the play had ended but the curtain had yet to come down.'"

Perhaps that is the attraction of the Yukon. It preserves things. It holds on. It keeps the past in cold storage, or at least revives it with contemporary adventure. "You don't hear the sound of the old paddlewheels anymore," lamented a retired constable in Whitehorse, "or the steam whistles blowing. It's all gone." But he said, "There's new people coming now. The old communities are gone, yes, but you go down that river today, and there's all kinds of boats on it. Canoes, kayaks, rubber rafts, dozens of them. They'll find the river again."

Adds native storyteller Louise Profeit-LeBlanc, "Knowledge of the people and the past, that's the gold of the 21st century."

And there's enough for everybody. ∎

SLED DOGS AND SURVIVAL — ALASKA

Siberian husky takes a break during an Alaskan sled-dog race. Dog mushing, once a way of life among Yukon River villagers, endures today more as a popular sport and recreation rather than as a necessity.

YUKON RIVER— NEAR DAWSON *Carrying boats in summer and snowmobiles in wint*

serves as a major thoroughfare for residents, who think little of gassing up and traveling many miles just to visit.

CITY OF WHITE HORSE Y. T.

ADAMS & LARKIN. PHOTO.
DAWSON Y.T.

THEN AND NOW—WHITEHORSE, YUKON TERRITORY

*Capital of Canada's Yukon, Whitehorse takes its name from the frothy white rapids
of the Yukon River, thought to resemble the manes of horses. While its
economy and other details have changed from a century ago—jet boats, for example,
now run where steamships once held sway—the town's topography remains
remarkably similar (opposite). Whitehorse still attracts spirited folk who love adventure,
storytelling, music, and their next-door muse, the Yukon River.*

MODERN MINING—YUKON TERRITORY

*One hundred years ago, miners could find gold nuggets in the stream gravels at their feet.
Today, more intensive techniques rule, such as using a water cannon to wash away a hillside (below)
and then sending the resultant slurry through a sluice box. It's a method that unearths and recovers
gold, but only at the expense of local streams and the riverine ecology.*

DAWSON, YUKON TERRITORY

*Riding tall atop his single horsepower carryall that requires neither tune-up nor tire change,
this Royal Canadian Mounted Policeman makes a distinguished presence in
Dawson (above), recalling days when the RCMP was the only authority in town. Yesterday's
stampedes of miners have lately given way to modern surges of summer tourists,
intent on experiencing the spirit of Dawson's storied past. While some local residents continue
to dredge gold—indeed, some bar tabs are still paid in gold dust—
trapping also remains a viable way of life.
One father-daughter team (opposite) displays part of a recent take, including wolf skins.
Trappers also seek beaver, marten, lynx, and other local furbearing species.*

YUKON FLATS NATIONAL WILDLIFE REFUGE — ALASKA

Braiding into a maze of channels and oxbows (above), the Yukon River feeds some 40,000 lakes and ponds within this 8.6-million-acre sanctuary near Fort Yukon, providing ideal summer habitat for some 30 species of waterfowl. Residents of Galena, Alaska, wager when spring breakup of the Yukon will occur; a clock fastened to the thinning ice (opposite) records the crucial moment.

FOLLOWING PAGES: SEAL HUNTERS — ALASKA

Yup'ik Eskimos from the village of Emmunak follow the middle mouth of the Yukon to the Bering Sea as they search for various species of seals, long a traditional source of meat, blubber, and skin.

MACKENZIE

ALEXANDER MACKENZIE

■ HE WAS, ACCORDING to some back home, "the man who ate his shoes," the courageous but unimaginative expedition leader who nearly died while walking five hundred miles across the snowy tundra of Arctic Canada in the dark and bitter December of 1821. Ten men starved to death under his command. One was murdered. Rumors of dissent and cannibalism persisted, all in a land where Inuit Eskimos lived comfortably. It was a tragic beginning to a career that would end with even greater tragedy. Yet once he returned to England he eagerly sought to redeem himself with a second expedition, and was granted his wish. So he left his young bride, whom he knew was dying of tuberculosis, and traveled again to Canada, taking with him the same blind optimism and easy disposition that would one day kill him and more than a hundred other men.

But on this warm August afternoon in 1825, beneath a great bowl of Arctic sky, John Franklin, age 39, plump and balding, stood on an island in the Mackenzie River Delta and, like most explorers of his day, considered his place in history.

Thirty-six years earlier, in July of 1789, a young Scotsman named Alexander Mackenzie had reached this point and become the first white man to navigate the river that would bear his name. Now Franklin hoped to carry the banner of exploration further, charting new Arctic coastlines and finding new opportunities for commerce. Perhaps he would even discover the Northwest Passage, that elusive— maybe mythical—route that in the minds of enterprising men would open lucrative trading lanes between the Atlantic and Pacific. Fighting back tears both of joy and grief, Franklin unfurled his dead wife's silk flag—he had learned by letter that she had died only six days after his departure from home—and buried it in the half-frozen soil. She had requested that he do this when he reached his prized objective.

It is a powerful presence to stand on the edge of distant lands and seas, the known and the unknown, the margins we find and create within and without us, the nexus of our own confidences and fears. And Franklin? Did he find comfort in seeing beluga whales in cold blue waters, their white flanks gleaming? Did he feel the weight of time pressing upon him, seeing skeins of geese going south, the August tundra turning russet with the advent of winter? Did he muse upon the snowy owl in its feathered perfection, or the eider drake lingering in summer's breeding plumage?

Drama had a way of shadowing John Franklin, but drama was no stranger in these high latitudes, where people had lived and died for as long as anybody could remember, following caribou, fish, geese, and the sun.

Alexander Mackenzie and his party tasted this land's drama when they pulled ashore near the mouth of the river and found four Inuit huts that, he wrote, "appear to have been inhabited during the last winter; and we had reason to think, that some of the natives had been lately there, as the beach was covered with the track of their feet." He noted runners and bars from their sledges, laid together near the huts, and pieces of netting "made of sinews, and some bark of the willow. The thread of the former was plaited, and no ordinary portion of time must have been employed in manufacturing so great a length of cord." Mackenzie also admired a "square stone-kettle, with a flat bottom…and we were puzzled as to the means these people must have employed to have chiselled it out of a solid rock into its present form."

Uncertain of his exact location in that maze of channels and islands that defined the mouth of the river, Mackenzie wrote that his guide "seemed to be as ignorant of this country as ourselves."

No wonder. They had traveled more than a thousand miles from Lake Athabasca to the Arctic Ocean on what the Natives called "Deh-Cho," the River Big. A broad waterway free of rapids and steady in disposition, Deh-Cho dropped only half a foot per mile. It provided easy travel—going downstream, at least—and ample fish and access to game. Yet it turned nasty when a stiff north wind confronted them, pushing against the strong current and creating big waves that could spill a canoe.

Two hundred and nine years after Mackenzie, I traveled his same river, but not by canoe. I went by jet boat and found myself wondering what I'd lost versus what I'd gained, roaring by mile after mile, fighting the clock and calendar, counting days, always in a hurry to get somewhere else. Always late. This wasn't my guides' fault, but my own, for I was the one with limited time to explore a long river.

We were a foursome, guides Loyal Letcher and Floyd Moses, both Dene Indians of the central Mackenzie, photographer Raymond Gehman, and myself. It seemed that whenever we needed to plan something we would motor ashore and build a fire, for in this cold and solitary country no decision could be made without one. Fire the companion, fire the muse. With the Mackenzie silently sliding by, always moving yet always there, we gathered driftwood, piled it high, dumped gas on it, threw a match, and jumped back. Whoosh. Flames licked the sky with columns of black smoke. None of that arduous Boy Scout stuff, down on our knees, whittling wood into tinder shavings piled for optimum combustion at the strike of a flint. This was the Dene way, Floyd told me with a wry grin, his dark eyes dancing. Start big and get bigger. Later, as a pool of warmth filled our camp, Floyd would set a metal grate over the crimson embers and top it off with a large coffeepot filled with river water. Only then could we discuss our options.

One night we camped just downriver of Fort Norman, roughly midway along the length of the Mackenzie, latitude 65 North. While Loyal and Floyd retired to sleep on the boat, Raymond and I pitched our tents on shore and stayed up late. The northern lights appeared overhead, pressing us to the ground as the green curtains reflected in the river that was blacker than the sky. Morning frost embroidered September's leaves and grasses, which had turned yellow and red in the growing cold.

TRADING POST — YUKON TERRITORY

*Relic of another era, the remains of an old Hudson's Bay Company trading post calls to mind
the transformational time when trappers entered Mackenzie country in the
early 19th century, changing forever the lives of the Indians they met. Often, trading posts
began as single dwellings and grew into modern towns.
For example, Fort Simpson — built at the confluence of the Liard and
Mackenzie Rivers, was called Liidli Kue by the Dene Indians,
meaning "where two rivers meet."*

The river swelled here, for just upstream the relatively short Great Bear River joined the Mackenzie from the west, where it flows out of Great Bear Lake. For two years during his second expedition, from 1825 to 1827, John Franklin and his party overwintered on the lake at a fish camp, now Fort Franklin. During the summers between, together with George Back and Dr. John Richardson, Franklin managed to chart more than 800 miles of the North American Arctic coastline, both east and west of the Mackenzie's mouth. Their accomplishment certainly wasn't the dreamed-of Northwest Passage, but it was significant enough to earn Franklin and Richardson knighthood.

By that time, white fur traders had arrived along the Mackenzie, and two powerful competitors, the North West Company and Hudson's Bay Company, had merged to rebuff the Russian-American Company that controlled the fur market along the continent's northwest coast and was looking to expand. Trading posts were built on the Mackenzie, every fifty to one hundred miles, usually at a confluence with a major tributary. In return for supplies and traps and guns traded to the Dene, white men would receive pelts of beaver, marten, muskrat, lynx, fox, wolf, and bear.

Fort Norman was built in 1810 across the river from a huge outcropping called Bear Rock, where legend says a native trapper staked three huge beaver pelts to its flank. People had always used this area for food, hunting caribou around Great Bear Lake and fishing the Mackenzie and Great Bear Rivers for arctic grayling. As I walked about the town of Fort Norman with photographer Raymond Gehman, pausing amid the strange hybrid of old and new—a teepee near a church, a dogsled near a pickup truck—I sensed my own peculiarities, being white and dressed too much like an outdoor clothing catalog. I should have looked more woods-wise; had more dirt under my nails and grease on my pants, or moose blood on my boots. It was September, after all, hunting season, when going to the meat market meant going into the woods with a rifle in one hand and a moose call in the other. Raymond and I bought ice cream at the local store.

Loyal and Floyd were moose hunters, always watchful for a big bull. Back on the river, even while traveling at 30 knots, they kept their high-powered rifles within arm's reach, somewhere under the peanuts and fruit drinks.

Near a place called Blackwater, upriver from Fort Norman, we pulled ashore where a traveler had a disabled skiff. Bad outboard, he said. Wouldn't run. His name was Tim Lennie. He and Floyd were buddies. They greeted each other like a pair of old shoes. Need any extra gas? Loyal asked him. Any tools, any help at all? No, Tim said. He was fine. He said that somebody would come along soon going his way (the opposite way we were going). Maybe a cousin or an uncle. Maybe tomorrow or the next day, or the day after that. Whenever. He invited us for coffee and something to eat. He had built a fire, and next to it a clever shelter made of driftwood and an old tarp. Beneath the shelter he had terraced the rocky shore into a suitable sleeping spot. When he laughed, and he laughed often, he threw his head back—and I could see that his mouth was mostly toothless. His long, obsidian hair framed an easy face and a radiant smile, and it was then that I realized this was not a predicament for Tim. He was in no hurry. He had no strict agenda or great expectations. He had probably traveled this river hundreds of times, winter and summer, frozen and free, and amid all the trials and trails in his life, this was simply no big deal. I suspected that he knew this river and its tributaries like the veins in his hand, and the faraway mountains like his bones.

Nowhere in America is there a highway—and certainly not an interstate—where if somebody's car breaks down, he or she just sits and waits on the side of the road for a cousin or an uncle to come by. Make a fire. Read a book. Watch the sun circumnavigate the summer sky, or the winter moon bathe the platinum, snowy hills of night. It warmed me to find somebody who was so patient in his world.

As is customary among people close to the land, Tim, Floyd, and Loyal spoke in stories instead of statistics. Floyd told about the time he and Tim and another guy flipped a skiff filled with four dead moose. "There we were...," Floyd recalled, traveling in the stern, the skiff biting into big waves but the riders unable to see beyond the huge pile of moose meat that filled the middle of the boat, unaware that the splashing waves were filling the bow. Suddenly the meat shifted forward and the bow-heavy skiff lurched up and over, flipping the men into the frigid Mackenzie. They nearly drowned, Floyd said, laughing. They stripped off their wet clothes and built a fire, then found the skiff and a can of gas and somehow got it going and made it home. Then there was the time Tim and Floyd camped on top of a mountain, and Floyd was hit by lightning. That didn't seem to bother him as much as later, when running down the mountain, he sprained his ankle. Then there was the time....

As I listened on and on to these people of the north, and watched them move in their sinuous and fluid ways, their weathered faces on the edge of fire and night, I thought again of Alexander Mackenzie, that stranger in a strange land who pondered an Inuit stone kettle in July 1789. That same month, halfway around the world in Paris—the so-called birthplace of Enlightenment and Reason—shopkeepers and artisans stormed the Bastille to protest the poverty of the masses, the persistence of serfdom, a thousand years and more of feudal corruption by the ruling class. None of these outrages existed among the Inuit who hunted caribou and built stone kettles. Yet Mackenzie had approached their world with trepidation. He was a long way from home, and in truth he didn't really know where he was. His guide said the Inuit were violent and "very wicked," that they had traveled south to raid and murder among the Dene people. The Inuit, according to modern historian and author Barry Gough, "lived in numerous local groups, always changing, that fringed Arctic waters from Greenland to Siberia. Migratory hunters, they roamed the lower Mackenzie area and were few in number."

Mackenzie slipped in and out of their world without mishap, and on September 12 he and his party arrived back at Fort Chipewyan, on Lake Athabasca, completing a round trip of nearly 3,000 miles in 102 days, not losing a man. He had wanted to go west, not north, where the river took him. But the Rocky Mountains had blocked his path. He had tried to persuade his guide to take him west, offering presents and bribes to no avail. "It is very certain that those People know more about the Country than they chuse to tell me," he wrote, adding that his chief guide, "being now & long since tired of the Voyage may occasion him to conceal from me part of what the Natives tell him for fear he should be obliged to undergo more fatigues—tho' he has always declared to me that he would not abandon me wherever I went."

Dene historian and politician Stephen Kakfwi has said, "Alexander Mackenzie came to our land. He described us in his journal as a 'meagre, ill-made people...people with scabby legs.'" And how might the Dene have described Mackenzie? Kakfwi said, "My people probably wondered at this strange, pale man in his ridiculous clothes, asking about some great waters [the Pacific Ocean] he was searching for. He recorded his views on the people, but we'll never know exactly how my people saw him. I know they'd never understand why their river is named after such an insignificant fellow."

Barry Gough adds, "The Dene continued to call their river Deh-Cho...in defiance of the official name as adopted by Canada. In its own way this difference represents the duality of historical understanding of contact and of occupation. On the one hand, Mackenzie may have been derisive, as Kakfwi suggests, in his remarks on the Dene. On the other hand, in its own

DENE INDIAN ARTISTRY

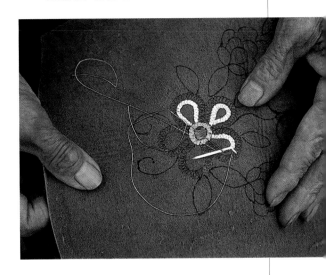

Embroidering with dyed porcupine quills, Sarah Hardisty—a Slavey Dene Indian from the community of Jean Marie River, on the upper Mackenzie—works a summer-flower design into a moose hide destined to become moccasins.

way, Kakfwi's remark belittles Mackenzie's own achievement, seeking as it does to portray him as a ridiculous stranger lost in Denendeh, the Dene homeland. Mackenzie himself never doubted his dependence on natives. His journeys across northwestern Canada depended on knowledge that he could gain only from natives. When such information was not available, however, as happened from time to time, he went on alone. He was not always on a guided tour."

Back in England, Mackenzie studied astronomy and navigation. He returned to Canada, and in 1793 breached the Rocky Mountains to become the first recorded white man to reach the Pacific overland. Knighted in 1802, he spent the rest of his years in distinguished comfort, mostly in London and Scotland, securing riches in the fur trade. The year before his death, in 1819, he wrote a letter to John Franklin, advising him in matters of logistics with canoes, guns, natives, and such. He ended, "If you can glean any thing from this that can assist you in the prosecution of your arduous undertaking it will be gratifying my anxious wish, as I feel earnestly interested in the results of your exertion under such perilous circumstances...."

Franklin survived that first expedition, barely. And his second was a success. But in the mid-1840s, while commanding two ships and a crew of 128 in search again of the Northwest Passage, he and all his men would disappear, never to be found. An expert in geomagnetism, a talented navigator, a likable man who author Pierre Berton has said, "literally wouldn't kill a fly," Franklin nevertheless failed to learn from the very natives whose homeland he explored. People had lived along Deh-Cho for thousands of years precisely because they did kill. For them, hunting and fishing wasn't sport. It was essential.

When, early in our trip, Loyal, Floyd, and I had stopped to meet Raymond in Norman Wells, site of the only oil refinery in the Northwest Territories, we quickly finished our business and hurried away. I found myself eager to leave the pipelines and helicopters and artificial islands built in the middle of the river, crowned here with drilling rigs. I later found a printed guide for canoeists that read, "Fresh drinking water may be taken from any of the streams emptying into the Mackenzie." Then added, "canoeists are advised that drinking water may be contaminated downstream from the oil development in Norman Wells."

Back on the river—the still-wild river—Loyal and Floyd finally got their moose, a young bull. Loyal smiled when he presented a leg of meat to his mother-in-law, and she smiled back, grateful.

The modern world has made inroads here. Near where Alexander Mackenzie pondered a stone kettle and John Franklin buried his dead wife's flag—at the mouth of a great river, all those years ago—the town of Inuvik now has commercial establishments with the names Polar TV, Arctic Rim Distributors, and Eskimo Inn. But everybody knows it isn't real. Places like that don't make wild Inuit or Dene dreams. For that you need to get on the river, sleep on the ground, make a fire. For that you need to tell stories and learn patience. ■

NORTHERN LIGHTS—NORTHWEST TERRITORIES

September campfire backlights a demonstration teepee on Cli Lake, near Fort Simpson, while the ever changing green curtains of the aurora borealis silently build and fade beyond.

HEADWATERS OF THE MACKENZIE — N.W.T.   *White pelicans summer on the Sla*

, near Fort Smith and the source of the Mackenzie River. Come fall, they migrate as far south as the coast of Mexico.

MACKENZIE MOUNTAINS — N.W.T. *September dusting of snow softens the hard pr*

the Cirque of the Unclimbables, 9,000-foot-tall granite prongs in the Ragged Range of the Mackenzie Mountains.

FORT GOOD HOPE — LOWER MACKENZIE

*Luminous amid autumn skies, Our Lady of Good Hope Roman Catholic Church (opposite) anchors
Fort Good Hope, a Slavey Dene Indian community of about 600 people who still live
largely by hunting, trapping, and fishing along the Mackenzie River. The church, built in 1865, boasts
a stunning interior (below) with murals hand painted by Father Emile Petitot and local
artists, who used fish oils and other natural ingredients to make their paints. Our Lady of Good Hope
remains one of the most popular tourist attractions of the entire Mackenzie Valley.*

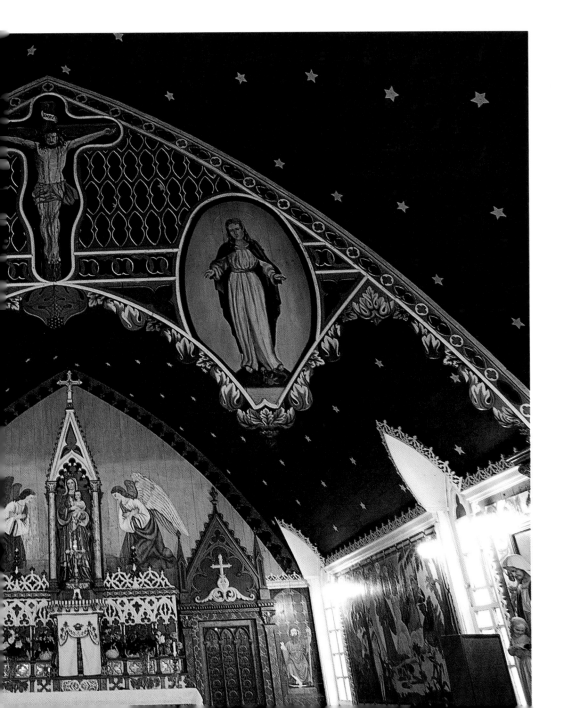

MACKENZIE RIVER DELTA—INUVIK, N.W.T.

*The village of Inuvik (above) lies along the lower Mackenzie near its mouth, where it branches
as it empties into the Beaufort Sea, part of the Arctic Ocean. Villagers here, as in most
Mackenzie River settlements, live with one foot in the traditional past and one foot in the uncertain
present, combining a subsistence existence with a modern cash economy. Among the
species still hunted both by men and polar bears, a bearded seal (opposite) suns itself on a beach.*

FOLLOWING PAGES: MOON AND THE RIVER

*Full moon rises over the Mackenzie Delta as days shorten and winter arrives. Soon the river's
waters will ice over, as the Mackenzie remains frozen for the next six months.*

Notes on the Contributors

Kim Heacox is author and photographer of four books on Alaska, and he wrote National Geographic's *Visions of a Wild America*, as well as *Antarctica: The Last Continent*. In addition to the Arctic and the Antarctic, he has covered Africa and the Galápagos. He has twice won the Lowell Thomas Award for excellence in travel journalism.

A longtime contributor to National Geographic publications, K. M. Kostyal most recently completed *Trial by Ice: A Photobiography of Ernest Shackleton* (October 1999). Her other books include *Stonewall Jackson: A Life Portrait* (Taylor 1999) and *Virginia: Art of the State* (Abrams 1999).

Paul Robert Walker, a former teacher and journalist, has written 16 books, including National Geographic's *Trail of the Wild West*. His work has been honored by the National Council for Social Studies, the Children's Book Council, the American Folklore Society, and *Storytelling World*. He lives with his wife and children in Escondido, California.

Freelance writer Mel White lives in Little Rock, Arkansas, and specializes in travel and natural history. He is a contributing editor for National Geographic *Traveler*, and has written for several other publications of the Book Division, including *Islands Lost in Time*.

Photographic Credits

Front Matter — 1 Jim Richardson; 2-3 Terry Donnelly; 4 Raymond Gehman; 5 (top left) Tomasz Tomaszewski; 5 (top right) Jim Richardson; 5 (bottom left) Michael Melford/The Image Bank; 5 (bottom right) Patrick & Baiba Morrow/First Light

Rivers to the Atlantic — 10-11 Tomasz Tomaszewski; 12 Brian Milne; 14 Painting by Theodore Gudin (1802-1879) in 1847, Versailles Castle, Giraudon/Art Resource, NY; 15 Archive Photos; 17 Bob Krist; 18-19 Bob Krist; 20 Tomasz Tomaszewski; 20-21 Daryl Benson/Masterfile; 22-23 Brian S. Sytnyk/Masterfile; 23 Tomas Tomaszewski/Visum; 24-25 Tomasz Tomaszewski/Visum; 26 Raymond Gehman; 28-29 Lycoming County Historical Society & Museum; 31 Mary Ann McDonald; 32-33 Raymond Gehman; 34-35 (both) Raymond Gehman; 36-37 Fred Habegger/Grant Heilman Photography, Inc; 38 Arents Collection, New York Public Library; 40 Winfield Parks; 43 James P. Rowan; 44-45 Chuck Savage/The Stock Market; 46-47 Medford Taylor; 48 David R. White; 49 Cameron Davidson/Tony Stone Images; 50-51 Medford Taylor

Rivers to the Gulf — 54-55 Jim Richardson; 56 Kimberly Parsons/Photo 20-20; 58 Archive Photos; 59 Courtesy of the Mariners Museum, Newport News, VA; 61 Gail Mooney; 62-63 Jim Richardson; 64 Jim Richardson; 65 Tom Till; 66-67 Michael Lewis/Photographers Aspen; 68 Phil Schofield; 69 Raymond Gehman; 70-71 Gail Mooney; 72-73 Jim Richardson; 74 National Archives; 76 The Granger Collection, N.Y.; 77 "Mih-Tutta-Hangkusch, A Mandan Village" after Bodmer, 1833, collection of Mr. and Mrs. Paul Mellon, photographed by Victor Boswell, Jr.; 79 Sarah Leen; 80-81 Sarah Leen; 82-83 (both) Sarah Leen; 84-85 Sarah Leen; 86 Sarah Leen; 87 Annie Griffiths Belt; 88-89 David

Hiser/Photographers/Aspen; 90 Tom Bean; 92 Dan Dry; 95 Ralph Lee Hopkins; 96-97 David Muench; 98 Tom Bean; 99 Ralph Lee Hopkins; 100-101 Michael Frye; 102 George H.H. Huey; 103 Willard Clay; 104-105 Bruce Dale

Rivers to the Pacific — 108-109 Michael Melford/The Image Bank; 110 Kerrick James; 112 Bruce Dale; 113 Peter Essick/Aurora; 115 David Edwards Photography; 116-117 Nevada Wier/The Image Bank; 118 David Hiser/Tony Stone Images; 119 John Russell/Network Aspen; 120-121 Ralph Lee Hopkins; 122-123 (both) David Edwards Photography; 124-125 Annie Griffiths Belt; 126 (left) Denver Art Museum, photographed by Lowell Georgia; 126 (right) Curtis Collection; 128-129 Smithsonian Institution; 131 Sarah Leen; 132-133 Woodward Payne/Photo 20-20; 134-135 Tom Myers; 135 Raymond Gehman; 136-137 (both) Sarah Leen; 138-139 Sarah Leen; 140 Tom & Pat Leeson; 143 Royal Ontario Museum; 145 Pat O'Hara; 146-147 Frank S. Balthis; 149 Natalie Fobes; 150 Jeff Gnass; 151 Ralph Lee Hopkins; 152-153 Jeff Gnass; 153 Jon Brenneis/Photo 20-20; 154-155 Jeff Gnass

Rivers to the Arctic — 158-159 Patrick & Baiba Morrow/First Light; 160 Jay Dickman; 162 Jeff Gnass; 165 Webster & Stevens; 167 Kim Heacox/Ken Graham Agency; 168-169 Jay Dickman; 170 Patrick & Baiba Morrow/First Light; 171 Jay Dickman; 172 Jeff Gnass; 173 Jay Dickman; 174-175 (both) Jay Dickman; 176-177 Jay Dickman; 178 National Gallery of Canada, Ottawa; 180 Raymond Gehman; 183 Raymond Gehman; 185 Raymond Gehman; 186-187 Raymond Gehman; 188-189 Raymond Gehman; 190-191 (both) Raymond Gehman; 192-193 (both) Raymond Gehman; 194-195 Raymond Gehman

Back Matter — 197 Raymond Gehman

Acknowledgments

The Book Division and the authors wish to thank the many individuals, groups, and organizations mentioned or quoted in this publication for their help and guidance. We are especially grateful to the following individuals: Lyn Clement, Pauline Desjardins, Dennis Deuschl, Randy Kane, John Lambertson, Ken Sinay, Tristan Smith, and Henry Sweets.

Additional Reading

Readers may wish to consult the *National Geographic Index* for related articles and books including: *Exploring America's Historic Places; Grand Canyon Country; Great Rivers of the World.* The following may also be of interest—

Atlantic: Quinn, David B., ed., *North American Discovery*; Stranahan, Susan Q., *Susquehanna: River of Dreams*; Woodlief, Ann, *In River Time*

Gulf: DeVoto, Bernard, ed., *The Journals of Lewis and Clark*; Havighurst, Walter, *Voices on the River*; Neider, Charles, ed., *The Autobiography of Mark Twain*

Pacific: Dietrich, William, *Northwest Passage: The Great Columbia River*; Parker, Kathleene, *The Only True People*; Powell, John Wesley, *Down the Colorado*

Arctic: *Alaska Almanac*, Alaska Northwest Books; Berton, Pierre, *The Arctic Grail* and *The Klondike Fever*; Gough, Barry, *First Across the Continent*

INDEX

Boldface indicates illustrations.

Fitting his body to his vessel, a canoeist partaking in the Susquehanna Sojourn '98 finds time for a siesta near the town of Ulster, Pennsylvania.

EXPLORING THE GREAT RIVERS OF NORTH AMERICA

Contributing Authors:
Kim Heacox
K. M. Kostyal
Paul Robert Walker
Mel White

Published by the National Geographic Society

John M. Fahey, Jr. *President and Chief Executive Officer*
Gilbert M. Grosvenor *Chairman of the Board*
Nina D. Hoffman *Senior Vice President*

Prepared by the Book Division

William R. Gray *Vice President and Director*
Charles Kogod *Assistant Director*
Barbara A. Payne *Editorial Director and Managing Editor*
David Griffin *Design Director*

Staff for this book

Tom Melham *Editor*
Greta Arnold *Illustrations Editor*
Suez Kehl Corrado *Art Director*
Victoria Garrett Jones *Researcher*
Carl Mehler *Director of Maps*
Sven M. Dolling *Map Research*
Michelle H. Picard *Map Production*
Tibor G. Tóth *Map Relief*
R. Gary Colbert *Production Director*
Lewis R. Bassford *Production Project Manager*
Richard Wain *Production Manager*
Sharon Kocsis Berry *Illustrations Assistant*
Peggy J. Candore *Assistant to the Director*
Kevin G. Craig *Staff Assistants*
Dale-Marie Herring

Manufacturing and Quality Control

George V. White *Director*
John T. Dunn *Associate Director*
Vincent P. Ryan *Manager*
James T. Sorenson *Budget Analyst*

Mark A. Wentling *Indexer*

Library of Congress Cataloging-in-Publication Data
Exploring the rivers of North America / prepared by the Book Division.
p. cm.
Includes index.
ISBN 0-7922-7846-1 (alk. paper). —ISBN 0-7922-7847-X (deluxe: alk. paper)
1. North America—Description and travel. 2. Rivers—North America. I. National Geographic Society (U.S.). Book Division.
E41.E96 1999
917.304'929—dc21
99-25185
CIP

The world's largest nonprofit scientific and educational organization, the National Geographic Society was founded in 1888 "for the increase and diffusion of geographic knowledge." Since then it has supported scientific exploration and spread information to its more than nine million members worldwide.

The National Geographic Society educates and inspires millions every day through magazines, books, television programs, videos, maps and atlases, research grants, the National Geography Bee, teacher workshops, and innovative classroom materials.

The Society is supported through membership dues and income from the sale of its educational products. Members receive NATIONAL GEOGRAPHIC magazine—the Society's official journal— discounts on Society products, and other benefits.

For more information about the National Geographic Society and its educational programs and publications, please call 1-800-NGS-LINE (647-5463), or write to the following address:

National Geographic Society
1145 17th Street N.W.
Washington, D.C. 20036-4688 U.S.A.

Visit the Society's Web site at www.nationalgeographic.com.